gym mom

The Twists and Turns of Your Daughter's Gymnastics Career

By: Rita Wieber

Published by USA Gymnastics
Indianapolis, Indiana

Enjoy the journey!

Cover art by Elliot Rudert.

Back cover portrait by Terri Shaver Photography.

ISBN: 978-0-615-64593-3

Published in the U.S. by
USA Gymnastics
132 E. Washington St., Suite 700
Indianapolis, IN 46204

dedication

For Jordyn.
one of many blessings in my life.

acknowledgments

Writing this book has not only been a joy, but the fulfillment of one of my dreams. My heartfelt thanks goes to all of those who have supported Jordyn and our family throughout the last 12 years, especially our friends and family.

Thanks to John and Kathryn Geddert and all of the wonderful coaches and staff at Gedderts' Twistars USA Gymnastics Club, who, through their expertise, caring and perseverance, helped Jordyn reach her full potential in the sport of gymnastics.

This book would not be possible without the support of the entire staff of USA Gymnastics, especially: Steve Penny, Luan Peszek, Leslie King, and Jeannie Shaw. A special thank you to Kathy Kelly and Martha Karolyi for their leadership, knowledge and caretaking of all of the U.S. national team gymnasts over the years.

I am grateful to the experts who graciously shared their knowledge and experience: Dr. Larry Nassar, Dr. Alison Arnold, Louise Whitney, RD, and Valerie Kondos-Field. A special thanks to Mary Lou Retton for her time and thoughtfulness, and to all of the gymnasts, gym moms, and coaches that provided invaluable feedback and information for this book.

I extend a special thanks to Sarah Marshall who provided her time as editor of the manuscript.

Last, but certainly not least, thanks to my loving and supportive husband, Dave, who deserves an award for being my husband for over 26 years. And to my precious children, without whom I'd be lost: Lindsay, Ryan, Jordyn and Kyra.

table of contents

introduction

T he phone call came while I was visiting a friend in London. After the annual group pre-team testing at Gedderts' Twistars Gymnastics Club our 5-year old daughter, Jordyn, was chosen to be part of a select group of gymnasts in an accelerated, competitive track program. My husband explained that this would mean nine hours of practice per week, up from the current three hours. "That is ridiculous," I replied. "She's 5 years old for crying out loud."

Jordyn at age 3.

That phone call was the beginning of a journey that would forever change our family dynamics. Little did I know that 10 years later Jordyn would be practicing 30 hours a week and traveling around the world competing for Team USA. From the beginning, an instructional guide to the world of gymnastics would have been handy. I was clueless about the wild, wonderful, sometimes wacky world of gymnastics.

Competitive gymnastics is multi-faceted, exciting and captivating. When your daughter's gymnastics talent is identified, it is natural to jump to grandiose thoughts of Olympic gold medals. If not careful, parents of gymnasts could find themselves as prime material for the next reality show. Television programs such as Dance Moms and Toddlers and Tiaras provide a peek into the extreme behavior of mom's who appear to be heading to the edge of reality because of their children's success.

From recreational to elite gymnast, the 12-year path of my daughter's gymnastics career served as a real-life education into a world I never knew existed. Those years taught me about the distinct personality of gym moms; the mental and emotional ups and downs of gymnasts; and moments of disappointment, injury and joy. They also demonstrated how athletes achieve lifelong dreams, amazing accomplishments, happiness and memories that will last a lifetime.

I did find myself heading in the wrong, possibly overboard, direction a number of times in dealing with coaches, other parents, and my daughter. This book is by no means a "how-to-succeed" guide. Rather, it is a collection of information, anecdotes, observations and lessons I learned along the way. The intention of this book is to provide gymnastics' mothers, fathers, grandparents, siblings, relatives and friends information about what may be ahead so they can make the most of the journey with their artistic gymnast.

The first of 10 chapters starts with a story of Jordyn's gymnastics journey. The next two chapters serve as a reference guide for recreational and competitive gymnastics. The following chapters advise how to interact with coaches and parents. Chapters 6 and 7 are full of useful information on keeping your gymnast healthy physically including interviews with registered dietician Louise Whitney and Dr. Larry Nassar, the U.S. Women's National Team physician. Chapter 8 delves into sports psychology including advice from Dr. Allison Arnold, clinical psychologist and consultant for USA Gymnastics. Chapter 9 completes the journey with life after club gymnastics, whether it is collegiate gymnastics, elite gymnastics or closing the gymnastics chapter in your daughter's life. Finally, Chapter 10 summarizes the life lessons I have learned along this incredible journey.

Participation in competitive gymnastics changes lives: it can affect the entire family, but with proper preparation and a solid foundation, the joy is immeasurable.

CHAPTER ONE

jordyn's journey

Jordyn on her first birthday– starting to get her "guns."

I t seems cliché to start with Jordyn's birth. Yet, I have a very vivid memory of feeling something different when Jordyn was born. Jordyn was my third child, born almost exactly 18 months after my son, Ryan. I was ecstatic when Jordyn was born, but I also had a strange intuitive feeling that this child would need me more than the others. It was a scary feeling. I'm still not sure if that feeling was an intuition of her future gymnastics career or something else. Nonetheless, the feeling was there.

When Jordyn was about 10 or 11 months old she started walking. Our other two children were also early walkers, but when Jordyn took off behind her push toy, we couldn't help but laugh at her muscular calves. Her genetic muscular build became more and more evident the more mobile she became.

During those early walking months, my husband, Dave, and I also noticed Jordyn seemed to have an extraordinary sense of balance. While we dressed the other children at the same age, they would stand on the dressing table and lean on our shoulders as we helped them step into their pants. Jordyn did this with no leaning, just one-legged balancing, almost pelican-like. Between the muscles and the balance, we decided Jordyn looked like a gymnast and that became our little phrase of endearment, "Oh, look at our little gymnast."

When Jordyn was two-and-a-half I decided to enroll her in a mom-and-tot gymnastics class at our local gym, which happened to be where she has spent her entire career, Gedderts' Twistars USA. Jordyn loved the obstacle courses, colorful mats and running around hopping and balancing as did all the kids. To be honest, I was surprised that the teacher never commented on Jordyn's muscles.

"Can't they see how muscular she is?" I thought. "All the moms in Jordyn's dance class would comment on her biceps. Why isn't the gymnastics teacher saying anything?" I remember thinking, "Maybe she's not our little gymnast after all." So, we took a couple of years off of gymnastics.

the recreational years

Jordyn's body kept growing and becoming more muscular and athletic looking. At age 4-and-a half we decided to try gymnastics again, this time in a recreational class. At Gedderts' Twistars Gymnastics Club, located only 15 minutes from our house, recreational sessions ran for eight weeks. Midway through the second eight-week session, Jordyn was moved up to the next level of recreational gymnastics. She was learning new tricks quickly, but was by no means the standout in her class. As the moms sat and watched the class, many would report to me that their daughter did back handsprings all over the house. Jordyn had yet to do a single back handspring.

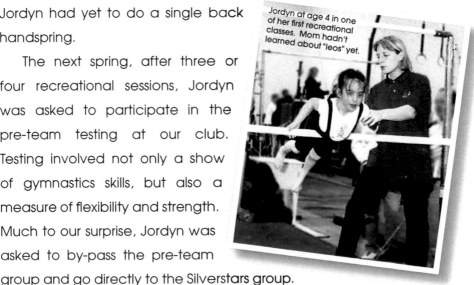

Jordyn at age 4 in one of her first recreational classes. Mom hadn't learned about "leos" yet.

The next spring, after three or four recreational sessions, Jordyn was asked to participate in the pre-team testing at our club. Testing involved not only a show of gymnastics skills, but also a measure of flexibility and strength. Much to our surprise, Jordyn was asked to by-pass the pre-team group and go directly to the Silverstars group.

At Twistars, the Silverstars was a hand-selected group of gymnasts who would follow the fast track into Level 5 competition with extra focus on conditioning. Selected by John Geddert himself, the owner of the gym and a national-caliber coach, invitation to the Silverstars group was considered an honor.

With four children, including a baby, I could not fathom getting Jordyn to the gym three nights a week. I was already struggling with two school-aged, active children. I decided to call John Geddert directly and ask him if Jordyn was really selected for her potential or just to fill a spot. John told me that Jordyn scored low in the skills and flexibility area but very high in strength. He said skills would be easy to teach with her strength and that flexibility can be developed. With John and Jordyn's persuasion, we decided to give it a try.

the junior olympic years

The Silverstars program was based on strength and skill building for 18 months before the gymnasts would be Level 5 competition-ready. During this time the girls trained for the Talent Opportunity Program (TOPs), USA Gymnastics national program of testing physical abilities and skills to identify future high-level talent. After regional and national testing, Jordyn earned the highest level of TOPs designation for age 7, the Diamond Level. Jordyn was the first athlete to attain this level in Twistars' history. We began to realize that she had some exceptional talent and were looking forward to the beginning of her competitive gymnastics career.

In January 2003, Jordyn competed in her first Level 5 gymnastics competition, our club's invitational. At age 7, in an award age group of 10-and-under, Jordyn didn't receive a medal and placed sixth in the all-around. In each subsequent competition that season, Jordyn

Jordyn's first official gymnastics picture – age 6

improved her scores and ended the season by tying for first at the state meet. After low scores in a few areas, Jordyn achieved the Gold level in TOPs in the 8-year old division.

The next year, at age 8, Jordyn remained a Level 5 gymnast for the early season and competed Level 6 from January to May 2004. She finished the season by placing second in the all-around at the Level 6 state championships.

The following fall, at age 9, Jordyn competed one meet at Level 7 and obtained the necessary score to move on to Level 8. She ended the season as the Level 8 regional champion. She also made the National A Team for the TOPs program, earning her a training camp at the Karolyi Ranch, the U.S. Women's National Team Training Center in Huntsville, Texas. That was Jordyn's first taste of "The Ranch," a place she would call her second home just a few short years later. Her progress that year convinced us that she had a serious future in competitive gymnastics.

After winning the Level 8 regionals, John identified a group of girls to place on an accelerated path toward elite gymnastics, training them twice a day for three days per week. This was relatively easy to negotiate in the summer but became more difficult when the school year began. For a middle school student, missing three hours of school each morning, three days a week was unchartered territory for our district. The district administrators agreed, as is detailed in a future chapter, and Jordyn handled the new, intense schedule very well.

That year, at age 10, Jordyn competed in one meet at Level 9, allowing her to move to Level 10 where she qualified for the Junior Olympic (JO) nationals and placed second in her age group. The gymnast who beat her was 14 years old. We were thrilled with her performance, and she was ready for more. TOPs testing was another success that year; Jordyn earned a spot on the National A Team and another training camp at the Ranch.

Just a few weeks after Level 10 nationals, at age 10, Jordyn qualified as an international elite gymnast. The next step was to travel to Kansas City for the U.S. Classic where she would attempt to qualify for the Visa Championships, USA Gymnastics' National Championships. With no expectations and very little pressure, we were thrilled and surprised when Jordyn qualified for the 2006 Visa Championships in St. Paul, Minn.

That first year at Visa Championships was probably the most exciting for all of us. At age 11 and one month, Jordyn was the youngest competitor. Once again, we had no expectations and were honored just to be at that meet. Jordyn was excited in her own intense way. I remember unpacking in our hotel room. She hung her new sparkly leotard and warm-up suit on a rack in the room, looked at me and said, "Mom, I love this."

The decision to allow Jordyn to attempt elite gymnastics at such a young age was not easy, but at that moment, I felt a sense of peace about it.

the elite years

Surprisingly, Jordyn made the 2006 U.S. Junior National Team by tying for ninth at championships. A spot on the team meant Jordyn now had the chance to vie for international assignments and compete for her country, as well as monthly five-day trips to the Ranch for National Team training camps. For me, this new status was thrilling and scary all at the same time. The thrilling part was Jordyn's elite career included signing her first autograph and discovering a fan page on the Internet. The scary part included the expectations placed upon her as an elite gymnast.

Jordyn did not receive a competition assignment that year because she was too young to compete at any of the international meets. Athletes had to be 12 to compete internationally. Unfortunately, due to her National Team status, she had to forego the trip to the U.S. Olympic Training Center in Colorado Springs, Colo., that she earned as a Level 10 National Team Member. The top four gymnasts from each age group at Level 10 Nationals earn this trip. Missing that trip was a bit sad for her; yet, she did have the opportunity to attend a special exchange camp where athletes from several other countries came to the Ranch to train. During this time, her coach John also had her compete in some of the larger invitational meets with the Twistars team. Her participation on the Twistars

Jordyn signing her first autographs at the 2006 Visa Championships.

team dismayed some of the Level 10 gymnasts' parents, who watched their daughters lose medals to an elite gymnast. It was a different year–bittersweet to say the least. While I could understand the perspective of the other parents, Jordyn's only opportunity to compete that year was in the Level 10 or open sessions at invitational meets.

The world of elite competition is very different from the Junior Olympic levels. Elite gymnasts only compete a handful of times each year. Gymnasts vie for assignments to meets. Not everyone is selected, and it's not unusual, depending on injuries, for an elite gymnast to not receive an assignment all year long despite being a member of the U.S. National Team. For an elite gymnast as young as Jordyn her coach had her compete in the Level 10/open meets because he thought it was important for her to gain more experience competing her higher-level skills.

In 2007, the Visa Championships propelled Jordyn to the podium. She placed third in the all-around behind Rebecca Bross and Samantha Shapiro. Shortly after the Visa Championships, Jordyn, who was now 12 and old enough to compete internationally, received her first international assignment, the Junior Pan American Championships in Guatemala. At the start of this elite road, I made a pact to do everything in my power to attend all of Jordyn's meets, regardless of location. I traveled to Guatemala and was the only parent who attended the event in a city under critical security status. Fortunately, because Jordyn was only 12 years old and I was the only parent attending, USA Gymnastics allowed me to stay in the same hotel as the athletes. I discovered this is not usually allowed so the athletes aren't distracted. Jordyn was very conscientious about not seeing me at all and following team rules. The U.S. Marines stationed in Guatemala provided the gymnasts with security protection. Between several nice Marines and the men's team judges,

We had this card created after Jordyn made her first U.S. National Team in 2006.

with whom I could socialize without breaking any rules, I had a great time on that trip. The team placed first, and Jordyn, who was second in the all-around, won gold on bars and beam, and placed third on floor. This trip made me realize what a great opportunity traveling would be for Jordyn. She would have the chance to experience areas of the world she might not otherwise see, all the while enjoying the sport she loves.

In February 2008, Jordyn was assigned to the Grand Prix Competition in Venice, Italy. Much safer than Guatemala, I took my older daughter, Lindsay, along with me and we enjoyed three days of site-seeing before watching the U.S. Junior Team win the team gold, and Jordyn win her first elite all-around title. She was then named to the Pacific Rim Championships team but withdrew due to an ankle sprain. This was her first real experience with disappointment due to injury.

Fortunately, Jo was healed and ready for the 2008 U.S. Classic and Visa Championships, where she became the U.S. junior national champion. She was on top of the world after that meet, and it warmed my heart seeing her achieve her goals.

The fall of 2008 started with a bang, as Jordyn traveled with the

U.S. junior national team to the Top Gym competition in Belgium. My husband traveled with me, and we enjoyed a little vacation and witnessed Jordyn earn the gold medal in the all-around, bars and beam.

Jordyn's first major title at a senior-level international meet came at the 2009 Tyson American Cup in Chicago. With a bit of controversy due to her age, Jordyn, then 14, completed her Amanar vault (a Yurchenko with two and one-half twists) for the first time and hit the rest of her routines to win the title. This meet proved to be extra special because our entire family was able to attend and support Jordyn. A trip to Montreal for the Gymnix International competition completed her competitive season that year, where she won the all-around, vault, bars, beam and floor titles.

SETBACKS

A couple of months after the Gymnix meet, I got a text from John while at work. "Jordyn tweaked her hamstring today." The "tweak" wound up being a relatively serious hamstring injury that kept her out of competition for 14 months. With the devotion and expertise of Dr. Larry Nassar, the U.S. Women's National Team physician, who happens to live in our hometown, Jordyn regained complete health and was ready to return to competition the following March. Jordyn was named to the 2009-2010 U.S. National Team without competing in the Visa Championships, and she was assigned to the 2010 Pacific Rim Championships in Melbourne, Australia.

Once again, my husband and I took the opportunity for a vacation. Jordyn was unable to perform some of her difficult skills due to junior competition rules. Nonetheless, the U.S. junior team won the gold and Jordyn earned the gold in the all-around, bars and floor. Seeing Jordyn return to competition after such a long rehabilitation period and then do so well brought tears to my eyes.

The 2010 U.S. CoverGirl Classic, considered a "warm-up" for the Visa Championships, was low-pressure and fun for Jordyn. She won the all-around, vault and bars gold medals. After missing the previous Visa Championships, she was chomping at the bit to get back and prove herself in Hartford, Conn. While at the Championships, I feared things were headed in the wrong direction when I opened the curtain in our Hartford hotel room to the beautiful view of a brick wall.

Despite my anxiety, Jordyn started the first day of competition by hitting her Amanar vault for her all-time high score of 16.00. My mind eased until I saw John Geddert scratching his head and pacing on the competition floor. I assumed it was just general nervousness. It wasn't until Jordyn fell on her release move on bars that I noticed the tape on both of her ankles.

The message somehow got to me that Jordyn had landed short on her beam dismount in warm-up just prior to competition and severely sprained both of her ankles. Dr. Nassar taped them, but the injuries proved to be too serious for her to perform beam. She mounted the beam anyway and almost instantly fell on her first tumbling series.

Devastated, I walked out of the arena to the corridor. It was too hard to watch. I had never left a competition before. I returned only to find that Jordyn had fallen two more times for a total of three falls. She was unable to finish the meet.

Jordyn later told me that the tape on her ankles prevented her from feeling the beam, but without tape, she had too much pain. This was the second time she missed championships!

An MRI on her ankles a few weeks later revealed a severe tear in one ankle. This news marked the beginning of several months of healing, rehab and no competition. On the positive side, Jordyn was granted a spot on the U.S. National Team even though she didn't finish the competition. I was relieved to think that the National Team Coordinator, Martha Karolyi, still had faith in her and knew Jordyn's falls on beam were not due to mental weakness, as was indicated in a few newspaper articles.

THE COMEBACK

After five months of healing, Jordyn was selected to compete at the 2011 AT&T American Cup. This year, the AT&T American Cup was an International Gymnastics Federation World Cup event, which means that only the top all-around athletes from the previous World Championships were invited to compete. The World Cup designation made the meet more prestigious. The top two U.S. athletes at the 2010 World Championships were Alexandra (Aly) Raisman and Rebecca Bross. Bross suffered an injury and would be unable to compete and Jordyn was selected to replace her.

The field included 2010 World All-Around Champion Aliya Mustafina of Russia and Aly Raisman of the USA. Jordyn started out with a small edge on vault, both she and Mustafina performed the difficult Amanar. After a fluky fall on bars, a win seemed out of the question, but Jordyn rallied with a near perfect beam routine and a nicely hit floor routine. Mustafina had a few wobbles on beam and then fell on floor, allowing Jordyn to win by a 0.06 margin. It was an incredible, unexpected victory that gave Jordyn a burst of confidence and excitement for the big, future challenges.

A few weeks later Jordyn returned to Venice, Italy, for the City of Jesolo Trophy competition. A less difficult routine on bars and a fall on floor left Jordyn in second place in the all-around. Coming back to the gym a bit tired, Jordyn was ready to focus on detail work and prepare for the U.S. CoverGirl Classic and Visa Championships in the summer of 2011.

Jordyn after winning the all-around title at the 2011 World Championships in Tokyo.
Photo by John Cheng.

At the U.S. CoverGirl Classic, used as a warm-up competition, Jordyn competed only on bars and beam, winning bars and tying for first on beam. One month later, Saint Paul, Minn. was the site of Jordyn's very first senior Visa Championships.

After day one, Jordyn was in first place but hungry for better execution after less than ideal performances on bars and floor. The second day proved to be the best competition of her career to that point posting a 61.450 in the all-around and winning the U.S. all-around title by more than six points. The hoopla of her first senior champion-ships win was short-lived. She left for the World Championships selection camp two weeks later.

2011 WORLD CHAMPIONSHIPS

The selection camp at the Ranch in Houston was business as usual. Jordyn did have a fall on floor but felt confident that she was on the right track. After an eight-day stay back home, she returned to the Ranch for the second selection camp where Martha Karolyi would announce the World Team after verification and a meeting of the selection committee. Verification is actually a "mock" meet where the athletes compete for a chance to earn an international assignment.

Despite a fall in her floor routine, Jordyn was named to the team along with Alicia Sacramone, Alexandra Raisman, Gabrielle Douglas, McKayla Maroney and Sabrina Vega. Anna Li was named the traveling alternate, and 2008 Olympic balance beam champion; Shawn Johnson was the non-traveling alternate. The team stayed at the Ranch for another five days of training before departing to Tokyo.

Blogs and Twitter posts assured us that practice was going well and the U.S. Team looked strong and determined. Then, the unimaginable happened when Alicia, the most experienced team member, suffered an injury in training and had to fly home for surgery on her Achilles' tendon.

The gymnastics websites and blogs began buzzing about the ability of the group of young gymnasts left to carry on without their mentor and captain. But the girls pressed on as a tribute to what Alicia had taught them about confidence and leadership.

My husband and I strategically booked our trip to Tokyo between two of our son's football games, which meant we would miss the qualifying round. This round determined who would advance to the team finals, all-around and individual event finals. One mishap and a top athlete could literally not participate in the medal rounds.

When Jordyn called from Tokyo at 2 a.m. Eastern Time, my heart

Jordyn with National Team Coordinator, Martha Karolyi. Photo by John Cheng.

jumped, as it does whenever the phone rings in the middle of the night. It's either really bad news or really good news. With the sound of both relief and excitement, Jordyn told me the U.S. Team had the highest qualifying score, and she qualified for the all-around, bars, beam and floor finals.

The knowledge that in the next few hours we'd be on our way to Tokyo for the World Championships made it hard to sleep the rest of the night. A puddle jumper to Chicago and a 12-hour flight later, we landed in Tokyo. I had a sense of peace knowing I was actually within walking distance of Jordyn.

Two nights, a few Sakis, and a little sushi later, we were finally in the

Tokyo Metropolitan Gymnasium for the team finals of the 2011 World Championships. Seeing Jordyn march into the arena with the team was the first time I saw her since she left for the second selection camp almost four weeks earlier. I had an instant sense of relief.

The team competition was brutal in the sense that there was no room for error. Three girls from each country competed on each apparatus, and all three scores counted. In many team competitions, as well as in the team qualifier, five girls compete but only four scores count. The pressure at the World Championship is so much greater because I did not want my daughter to have the fall that cost the team a medal. I'm not sure if the girls felt that sense of pressure, but this mother sure did.

The U.S. Team started on vault, an event that we tend to dominate. Jordyn, Aly and McKayla all nailed their vaults giving the U.S. a hefty lead going into the second rotation.By the time the girls rocked on bars and beam, we were a solid four points ahead of the Russian team. It would literally take a fall on floor from every girl, and then some, to lose the team gold.

Watching McKayla, Jordyn and then Aly confidently complete their floor routines was probably the most fun I've ever had at a gymnastics meet. Seeing the girls celebrate together, knowing that they had overcome losing a teammate to injury was a moment I will never forget. I'm not much of a crier, but I shed some tears during that award ceremony.

The celebration that followed with the whole USA group was a night to remember. This was only the third time the U.S. Women had won the team gold in the history of gymnastics. I don't think I've ever seen Jordyn happier.

That glow carried my husband and me through another 48 hours until we were back at the arena for the all-around finals. Jordyn and Aly were the two American women who qualified. The biggest threats were Viktoria Komova of Russia and the Chinese gymnasts. I took my handful of good luck charms and started pacing, leaving my husband, Dave, to sit with the other parents.

The girls started on vault once again. Jordyn hit, with a large step that cost her a couple of tenths of a point, but still left her in the lead after one rotation. Bars were a different story. Jordyn missed a connection that cost her an entire point while Komova and both Chinese gymnasts hit huge routines. Jordyn dropped to fourth place. At that point, I went outside, sat on the steps of the arena and told myself, "So, she won't win. Life will go on. She will learn from this and just want it more." I clutched my charms and went back in for more pacing.

Nine years ago, beam was the only event where I became nauseously nervous. In the world of elite gymnastics, they were all equal. This beam routine was an exception. While the routine only lasts a minute and a half, it seemed like an eternity. Before my mind got through every possible outcome scenario it was over, and it was nearly perfect. Her score pulled her into second place. At this point, a medal of any color would have been awesome.

Jordyn's floor routine was before Komova's routine, the Russian who held the lead by just more than four tenths of a point. Despite going out of bounds on one pass, Jordyn's routine was one of her best. The out of bounds error cost her one-tenth of a point deduction giving her a 14.800. Komova would need a 14.366 to win the gold. Surely, it was a done deal. The Russian's floor routine came with a couple low and shaky landings but it was a hit routine.

I was sitting alone when I saw the score flash –14.333. "Wait a minute, wasn't there supposed to be a six in there? It couldn't be!" Before I could do the mental math, I saw the screen flash the leader list. Jordyn was now on top!

That moment was one that I would love to freeze and repeat over and over. I later found out and saw on many YouTube videos the raw emotion that Jordyn experienced when she saw her name atop that leaderboard. She has never really explained to me what she felt during the meet. Maybe she will some day. For now, I will let that be her personal moment.

After finishing up two more days of competition for event finals, Jordyn headed home with her two gold medals and a bronze on beam. After a few days of celebration and rest, she was back at the gym working on her next dream.

My role as the mom continues: keep her grounded, feed her, shield her from unnecessary distractions, be sure she's rested, and love her unconditionally. Of course, if it were that easy, I wouldn't have been compelled to write this book.

CHAPTER TWO
gymnastics 101

When I was a child in the early 1970s, playing back yard kickball was a nightly neighborhood event. My parents transported me to dance class once a week. Basketball practice in middle school was merely one hour a week. There was no Internet, cell phones or Nintendo. There were only three television channels. We had nothing to do but play.

Times have changed. Kids today have countless choices for how to spend their free time. For those who can escape the lure of their computers, cell phones and video games, there are literally hundreds of sports and physical activities from which to choose. Why, then, choose gymnastics?

At the toddler and pre-school age, enrolling a child in gymnastics is an obvious choice. The environment is colorful and big. Kids can run, jump, roll, swing, hang and flip – all the things they aren't supposed to do

Jordyn at age 5 on a family trip to Florida.

in the living room. Recreational classes are usually set up in six- or eight-week sessions, making it affordable without a long-term commitment. Groups are usually small enough to keep a tight reign on energized kids who finish each class fulfilled and tired. What's not to love?

Even at this young age, kids get the chance to experiment with the traditional gymnastics equipment: balance beam, uneven bars, and vault. Classes for the toddler and preschool ages are geared toward physical activity, motor development, coordination, listening and following directions, discipline, strength, flexibility and self-confidence. As kids grow in age and strength, the sport becomes more specialized. Often between the ages of 6 and 10, gymnasts reach a pivotal fork in the road when they choose between recreational and competitive gymnastics.

recreational vs. competitive gymnastics

Deciding to pursue the competitive route is not an easy decision. Although the difference between recreational and competitive gymnastics is considerable, obviously, no decision is ever permanent. To put it simply, competitive gymnastics involves competition, and recreational gymnastics usually does not.

The purpose of a recreational program is to provide children with the physical, social, intellectual and emotional benefits that come from any activity program. Gymnastics skill can lend itself to any type of future athlete, who will benefit from gaining strength, speed and flexibility. While a recreational gymnast can reap those rewards, once your child is addicted to living life upside down, you may need to decide to make the switch to competitive gymnastics.

All gymnastics clubs do not do things the same way. At Jordyn's gym, Gedderts' Twistars USA Gymnastics Club, a pre-team testing day is held each spring for the upcoming fall. Girls are tested in flexibility, strength and skill categories, and then, recommendations are made for the next step. Since learning new skills safely requires a certain degree of strength and flexibility, the recommendation of a coach is desirable. Yet, if your child has the dream of competing in gymnastics and a coach has not approached you regarding that path, by all means, set up a meeting to discuss her goals.

Recreational vs. Competetive Gymnastics

HOW DO I KNOW IF MY CHILD SHOULD MOVE TO COMPETITIVE GYMNASTICS?

Children who enjoy competitive gymnastics crave challenge. A successful competitive gymnast does the skills and does them well. That is the basis of compulsory levels of gymnastics in the Junior Olympic or JO program. In front of judges, every gymnast does the same routine, and the prize goes to the one who performs the best. Getting better requires many hours of hard work and repetition. Gymnastics is not a sport for the mild or meek. It is a sport for the athlete hungry for the challenge.

HOW WILL THINGS CHANGE AFTER THEY SWITCH FROM RECREATIONAL TO COMPETITIVE GYMNASTICS?

Competitive gymnastics requires major commitment, both from the gymnast and to the team. Levels 3 and 4 require less than 10 hours a week. Training hours increase at each level and typically involve from 15 to 25 hours of practice per week. This leaves little time for other sports and activities and sacrifices have to be made. Missing practice frequently for other activities or sports means less consistency with training, and can ultimately lead to injury or disappointment. Gymnasts must understand the commitment before plunging into competitive gymnastics. Understanding expectations is important to avoid taking a spot on the team only to quit a short time later.

DO RECREATIONAL GYMNASTS COMPETE?

Coaches of competitive gymnasts are highly trained and focus on technique and moving an athlete to a higher level of competition. The main priority of recreational gymnastics coaches may not be technique...

DO RECREATIONAL GYMNASTS COMPETE? continued

...or skill development. Some recreational gyms develop a beginning competitive program and compete in "fun meets" at the very beginning levels of the Junior Olympic program, but progressing beyond that requires a gym that is set up for a competitive program. Specific Olympic-caliber gymnastics equipment is required that a recreational gym may not own.

While most gymnastics centers offer recreational classes, not every gym offers the competitive option. Competitive gymnastics is an expensive undertaking for the gym owner, requiring highly trained coaches, costly competitive-grade equipment, huge time commitment, and a lot of space. Moving to a gym with a competitive program might be necessary if that is the ultimate goal of your gymnast. There are hundreds of competitive gymnastics clubs registered with USA Gymnastics, the national governing body for the sport of gymnastics.

Choosing a gym should not be a quick decision. There are many factors that impact the gymnast's career. A convenient gym location should not be the top priority. If there is a good, competitive gym within a reasonable distance, count your blessings. At the higher competitive levels, it is not unusual for families to travel one or two hours to get to a top-notch gym. If your gymnast is considering a potential college scholarship as the prize, a few years of commuting to a better gym may be worth it in the long run.

Depending on location, not everyone has a choice in selecting a gym. Aside from community education programs or youth classes at athletic clubs, the Lansing area had two gymnastics clubs from which to choose when Jordyn was little. I called both clubs to get information on schedules and costs, and ended up choosing the club that was closest to our home. Fourteen years later, we are still at the same gym. We got lucky.

THE BASICS OF COMPETITIVE GYMNASTICS

The term gymnastics can refer to one of seven disciplines: men's artistic, women's artistic, rhythmic, trampoline, aerobic, acrobatic and Gymnastics for All. The International Gymnastics Federation (FIG) founded in 1881 in Belgium governs these seven disciplines worldwide.

The most popular of the disciplines is artistic gymnastics for men and women. The men's apparatus are floor exercise, pommel horse, still rings, vault, parallel bars and horizontal bar. Women's artistic gymnastics includes vault, uneven bars, balance beam and floor exercise, as described in this chapter.

The life of this gym mom has revolved around artistic gymnastics. Yet, while I know absolutely nothing about rhythmic gymnastics, trampoline, or even men's gymnastics, many of the tips and ideas presented in this book may be helpful to the mom of any gymnast or any competitive athlete.

CHOOSING A COMPETITIVE GYM

What to look for when choosing a gym:

- Lots and lots of mats. The gym should be large enough for equipment to be spaced adequately. There are requirements in the United States for gymnastics facilities to have their apparatus adequately spaced, inspected and secured. Mats should be placed around all equipment. Edges of equipment should be wrapped with padding. Many clubs offer a foam pit, tumble track and spring floor.

- No moldy mats. Be sure the gym looks and smells clean.

- No jiggling or rusty equipment. Old, unmaintained equipment could be dangerous. Be sure the gym is safe and the equipment is up to date.

- Coaches who pay attention and know what they are doing. Are they safety certified and background checked? Have they taken any coaching classes or training? Fluke accidents or injuries can happen to anyone. However, a coach must learn how to spot and how to teach so that an athlete can safely learn a skill. Coaches should also know how to handle an emergency injury situation. A neck injury can become life threatening quickly if not stabilized.

- A viewing area for parents. The decision of whether or not to watch your gymnast train is a separate issue, but there should be a safe, comfortable area for parents to watch if desired. Some parents feel more comfortable knowing they have the option to watch if they so choose.

- A coaching style that works for your child. It is a good idea to visit the gym and watch a practice or two before your child participates or ask for a trial practice. Some coaches are huggers and some are yellers. Some have athletes sit out if they are not working hard enough, others punish with more work. Be sure you and your child are comfortable with the coach's style and approach.

- An organized business. Be sure the gym has a method of communication that works for you. Little irritations such as not knowing if class is cancelled, not having a contact person to ask questions, or not knowing the meet schedule, can be frustrating.

- A good reputation. As with most businesses, positive word-of-mouth feedback proves most valuable.

USA GYMNASTICS

In the United States, USA Gymnastics is the national governing body for gymnastics (see inset).

As a gym mom, the USA Gymnastics website (**www.usagym.org**) is the best resource available for information on Junior Olympic or elite gymnastics. It was many years into Jordyn's gymnastics career before I was aware of USA Gymnastics and the tremendous benefits the organization provides. One click on this website leads you to resources on anything imaginable in the world of gymnastics; including the history of gymnastics, gymnastics archives, education, event information, photos, videos, and links to anything related to gymnastics.

JUNIOR OLYMPIC PROGRAM

Currently, Junior Olympic (JO) gymnastics is divided into two main divisions; compulsory and optional. At the time of this writing, the system is being restructured to include five compulsory levels and five optional levels. Details are still in the works. The program will be initiated in June, 2013. What follows is a description of the JO program as it currently exists, and the system that Jordyn followed through her career. Information on the new system will be provided by USA Gymnastics and will be available on their website (**www.usagym.org**) in the near future.

COMPULSORY LEVELS

Junior Olympic (JO) gymnastics has three segments, developmental, compulsory and optional. To advance from one level to the next, specific requirements for advancement must be met.

Levels 1 through 3 are considered developmental in nature and are not always included with competitive programs. These levels may be

Begin Here. Go Anywhere.

USA GYMNASTICS is the sole national governing body for the sport of gymnastics in the United States, designated by the International Olympic Committee and the International Gymnastics Federation. USA Gymnastics sets the rules and policies that govern gymnastics in this country. Training and selecting the U.S. Gymnastics Teams for the Olympics and World Championships are just two of the many responsibilities of USA Gymnastics.

USA Gymnastics is a non-for-profit organization and was established in Tucson, Ariz., in 1963. During the mid-1960s the U.S. had scarcely 7,000 athletes competing a limited schedule. The only major international events for gymnasts were the Olympic Games and the Pan American Games. In the last 50 years, the sport has grown by leaps and bounds.

Today, more than 110,000 athletes are registered in competitive programs through USA Gymnastics. USA Gymnastics has close to 20,000 professional and instructor members. Approximately 4,000 competitions and events throughout the U.S. are sanctioned annually. USA Gymnastics is headquartered in Indianapolis, Ind., and the original staff of three has now grown to more than 50 employees.

Gymnastics is a great foundation for children. It builds strength, flexibility, coordination, and confidence, just to name a few. Children of all ages can enjoy and benefit from the sport.

To locate a gymnastics facility in your area or for more information about any of the USA Gymnastics programs including Men's, Women's, Rhythmic, Acrobatic Gymnastics, Trampoline and Tumbling, or Gymnastics for All, visit USA Gymnastics' website **www.usagym.org**. You can also find a gymnastics facility in your area!

WOMEN'S GYMNASTICS EVENT DESCRIPTIONS

VAULT

The vault is actually a specially made table or platform. In 2001, the vault table was remodeled to be wider, longer and safer than the previous model. Since the change, gymnasts have performed more difficult vaults.

After running down a 25 meter runway, the athlete jumps on the springboard, performs some kind of an entry onto the table with his or her arms, pushes or "blocks" off the table and completes the vault by landing in a variety of positions. Popular entries to the table include a Yurchenko, or a round-off entry to the springboard; a front handspring entry directly from a jump off the springboard; or a Tsukahara, which includes a twist onto the vault table. From the table, the gymnast then tucks, maintains a straight body, pikes or twists to complete the vault by landing on his or her feet on a mat. The more twists and saltos (a fancy term for a somersault), the more difficult the vault.

The vault lasts about 10 seconds. As a mom, I consider any vault where the gymnast lands on the feet to be spectacular. A judge, on the other hand, factors body, arm, and trunk positions and height. In Junior Olympic gymnastics (up to Level 10), vault scores begin with a 10.0 or less depending on the difficulty and then deductions are made from that starting point.

UNEVEN BARS

The uneven bars consist of two fiberglass bars covered in wood laminate set horizontally at different heights. At the higher gymnastics levels bar routines are unique to each gymnast based on her skill level. Moves on the bars include moving from the low bar to the high bar and vice versa; release moves off the bar and catching it again; pirouetting or turning while in a handstand position; and dismounting in a flipping or twisting motion to the ground.

Once again, the more difficult the routine, the higher the value. Deductions are taken for things such as handstands that are not straight, bent arms, crooked pirouettes, pauses in the routine and falls.

BALANCE BEAM

Despite the illusion that gymnasts appear as though they are walking on flat ground the balance beam is only four inches wide and a little more than four feet high. While a beam routine lasts for a maximum of 90 seconds, for me, the routine seems to last for hours.

Beam rules and requirements become more challenging as the levels progress. For example, the gymnast must cover the entire length of the beam, and the routine must include both acrobatic and dance moves, at least one turn of 360 degrees, and a split leg leap. Some of the moves must be performed in a series of two or more elements. Of course, every bobble, wiggle, balance check or fall takes points off of the starting value. During beam routines, many spectators and even gymnasts hold their breath for the entire performance. That said, there is nothing more exciting than a hit beam routine.

FLOOR EXERCISE

One of the biggest thrills for a gymnast is progressing beyond the compulsory levels of gymnastics. At Level 7 and higher, gymnasts finally have a custom-made floor routine. Gymnasts can choose their own music and express themselves by contributing to the choreography. Floor exercise gives the athlete a chance to perform with some flair, get the audience involved with clapping and cheering, and tumble up a storm.

As with the other events, there are requirements to receive full credit. The routine, which may not last more than 90 seconds, must cover the entire floor. Depending on the level, certain leaps, turns and tumbling passes are required.

As with all events, sometimes a gymnast will perform a crowd-pleasing routine that looks great to the layman's eye only to receive a low score for deductions that only the judges notice. This is a reality of the world of gymnastics.

REGIONAL DIVISIONS

REGION 1
Northern California
Southern California
Nevada
Arizona
Utah

REGION 2
Hawaii
Montana
Washington
Oregon
Idaho
Alaska

REGION 3
Arkansas
Colorado
Kansas
New Mexico
Oklahoma
Texas
Wyoming

REGION 4
Iowa
Minnesota
Missouri
North Dakota
South Dakota
Wisconsin

achievement-oriented with a pre-team philosophy or as an introductory competitive program. Some states offer state championship meets for Levels 1-3, others do not.

A competitive gymnast does not have to start with Level 1 or any of the non-competitive/developmental levels. That being said, an athlete must be able to adequately complete the skills at Level 4 before qualifying to compete at Level 5.

The routines required at Levels 1-6 are all compulsory. This means that the routines are the same for every gymnast at their respective level. There are age limits and specific scores called "mobility scores" that provide eligibility for an athlete to move up, which must be obtained before progressing to the next level.

Individual gyms may also incorporate their own mobility score before an athlete is allowed to progress to the next level.

Many programs consider Level 4 or 5 to be the entry level for competitive gymnastics.

The competitive season for Levels 4–6 culminates with a state championship meet. An athlete must qualify for the state meet at one of several qualifying meets hosted by various clubs. Awards are then given to teams and individuals as well for the all-around score and each individual event.

REGION 5
Michigan
Illinois
Indiana
Ohio
Kentucky

REGION 6
Connecticut
Maine
Massachusetts
New Hampshire
New York
Rhode Island
Vermont

REGION 7
Washington DC
Delaware
Maryland
New Jersey
Pennsylvania
Virginia
West Virginia

REGION 8
Alabama
Florida
Georgia
Mississippi
North Carolina
South Carolina
Louisiana
Tennessee

XCEL (FORMERLY KNOWN AS PREP OPTIONAL PROGRAMS)

The Xcel or Prep-Op program, basically an alternative that exists outside of the Junior Olympic program, is designated for a gymnast who wants to perform optional routines at a competitive level, yet does not desire the rigor of the traditional competitive schedule, or has no desire to progress up through the levels. Xcel can be a stepping-stone for those gymnasts who have progressed beyond Level 6 but are not ready for Level 7 competition. Not all gyms offer Xcel programs.

OPTIONAL LEVELS

The final segment of competitive gymnastics in the Junior Olympic program is the optional Levels 7–10. Level 7 is the first taste of optional gymnastics, allowing tailor-made routines and competitive opportunities up to a state championship. There are difficulty restrictions at Level 7 and 8, as opposed to Levels 9 and 10 where the gymnast can perform any skill.

Beginning at Level 8, athletes can qualify from the state championship meet to a regional championship to culminate the season. Some regions conduct Level 7 regionals and prep opt/Xcel regional meets. USA Gymnastics has divided the states into eight regions. While it is not necessary to memorize what states are in each region, gymnasts are aware of their state's region, which may provide special camps, banquets or other activities.

Jordyn was well aware of gymnastics regions when she was in fourth grade. One day, I received a call from her teacher to relay a response that Jordyn gave in class. They were reviewing geography in Social Studies, and the teacher asked if anyone knew what region Texas was in. Jordyn confidently raised her hand and responded, "Region 3." Her teacher was confused, since she was looking for a response such as "the southwestern region." It became clear that day that gymnastics really was the first thing on Jordyn's mind.

Similar to Level 8, Levels 9 and 10 both include a regional championship meet where athletes can qualify for a Junior Olympic national championship meet. The national championship meet at Level 9 is split into East and West divisions, while Level 10 has one national championship for all states.

JORDYN'S PROGRESS THROUGH J.O.

AGE/GRADE	YEAR	SEASON	LEVEL	CHAMPIONSHIPS
6/ 1st	2001	Fall-winter	Training for Level 5	
7/ 2nd	2002	Fall	Training for Level 5	
7/ 2nd	2003	Winter	Level 5	States – TIE 1st AA
8/ 3rd	2003	Fall	Level 5	Early States – 1st AA
8/ 3rd	2004	Winter	Level 6	States – 2nd AA
9/ 4th	2004	Fall	Levels 7/8	
9/ 4th	2005	Winter	Level 8	States –1st AA Regionals –1st AA
10/ 5th	2005	Fall	Level 9	
10/ 5th	2006	Winter	Level 10	States – INJURED Regionals – 4th AA Nationals – 2nd AA

As with all levels of gymnastics, awards are given based on age-group divisions within the level. The division of the age groups is typically dependent on the number of gymnasts at the meet and to keep groups relatively even in size. For example, in a given year, there may be an extraordinary number of Level 10 gymnasts born in a given year, and this particular year may be broken down into several groups to allow more athletes to receive awards. Nonetheless, winning a national championship title in your age group at Level 10 ranks you among the best in the country and practically locks the chances for a college scholarship.

CHAPTER THREE
the addiction

Every bed became a trampoline in the early years.

The panic I felt learning Jordyn would initially practice nine hours a week was soon overshadowed by the shock of learning the cost of our precious daughter's new addiction to this sport. The nine hours a week quickly became 20 hours, then 23, then 30 hours a week. The time commitment was only the tip of the iceberg. Once Jordyn began competing regularly at age 7, we carefully made adjustments to the dynamics of our family, our finances, and our free time, to keep things balanced.

the bottom line—
the cost of gymnastics

In 1993 I quit my full-time job as an exercise physiologist. With four children, money and time had to be carefully managed.

One month of gymnastics tuition was about three times what we paid for our other kids to play any recreational sport for an entire season. Add the booster club dues, traveling costs, and competitive apparel costs and our budget became quickly unbalanced. Whenever my husband questioned the cost, I reminded him that gymnastics was much cheaper than figure skating or hockey. We were lucky!

Fortunately, my professional expertise lent itself to working several part-time and side jobs that I could schedule around the busy lives of my four kids. With lots of work, we made the gymnastics costs work.

BOOSTER CLUBS

Like many gymnastics clubs, our gym has a booster club that helps keep the cost of our gymnastics reasonable by providing financial assistance to the gymnastics families. Our booster club helps offset coaching fees at meets, entry fees and summer camp. The booster club's biggest fundraiser involves hosting an annual gymnastics invitational. Each family is required to participate on one invitational committee and work 20 hours at the event.

I quickly learned to reserve the weekend of our annual invitational. I really enjoyed working at the invitational because it brought so much joy to so many gymnasts. Seeing them compete with such confidence and pride was worth all the hard work. In fact, I received such a rush from the event that I volunteered to serve as meet chairperson one year. My husband participated in the meet by chairing the scoring system for several years. The meet provided a great sense of accomplishment and joy.

FUNDRAISERS

Our club had numerous fundraising opportunities that we took advantage of to help defray the cost of booster club fees. At first, I was gung-ho about the idea of fundraising. While for the most part I recommend fundraising, I am not sure how profitable it was for me.

For example, one time we were doing a pizza kit fundraiser. For each kit sold, the gymnast would get credit on her booster club dues. I solicited our friends and families and came up with an order for about 20 kits. At some point I realized that these kits were frozen, and unless I could deliver them to everyone on the same day, they needed to be stored in a freezer. Our side-by-side refrigerator could barely hold one frozen pizza, never mind 20 large pizza-making kits. Three hundred dollars later, I unloaded my kits into my brand new storage freezer with space to spare. I never ventured into fundraising again, although it is a viable option for many of my gym mom friends.

GYMNASTICS STUFF – NEEDS AND WANTS

About two minutes after realizing Jordyn was, in fact, addicted to gymnastics, I started hearing that giant sucking sound. The sound of money being sucked out of my wallet and into the hands of anyone who sold a product with the word "gymnast" or "gymnastics" on it. We bought key chains, blankets, bags, t-shirts, hoodies, sweatpants, underwear, necklaces, charms, posters, pillowcases and towels.

In reality, this was more my addiction. I, more than Jordyn, craved the excitement I felt whenever I found a new "gymnastics" labeled product. To be honest, if I could go back to the day when she was satisfied with a $15 "gymnastics" fleece blanket rather than the big-ticket items she wants now, I would.

While it is hard to resist the vendor tables at meets, we tried to limit our gymnastics product purchases to gifts or rewards. Needless to say, we have accumulated quite a collection of gymnastics items over the years.

GRIPS AND WRIST SUPPORTS

Starting at about Level 6 or 7, competitive gymnasts usually start wearing grips on their hands while working on the uneven bars. Grips are basically a strip of leather that covers the palm of the hands and connect with a velcro or buckle strap around the wrist. Gymnasts usually wear a terry cloth wristband under the grip strap for comfort. Grips help with holding on to the bar as well as reducing the severity of skin rips (see Chapter 7). While optional, most competitive gymnasts in the United States use grips. It is not unusual, however, to see gymnasts from other countries without grips or even chalk on the bars.

Many coaches are very specific about what type of grips they recommend for their gymnasts. The important thing is for the grips to feel comfortable to the gymnast. Grips come in different sizes and also need to fit correctly. A grip that is too long or too wide can be uncomfortable and even dangerous. Popular brands of grips include Ten-O, Bailie, Reisport and Jordyn's favorite, U.S. Glove with the single buckle. Grips range between $30 and $45.

Like a pair of leather shoes, grips need to be "broken-in" by initially wearing them for shorter amounts of time on easier skills and then gradually progressing to longer periods of time and more difficult skills. This is the reason gymnasts need at least two pairs at all times. Grips do wear out and can break at inopportune times.

Grips come with instructions on storage, which typically involves storing them in a separate clean bag. Grip bags, in fact, were one of Jordyn's favorite purchases at meets. Crafty people can create drawstring grip bags in all kinds of fabrics and designs.

You will also see gymnasts spraying their grips with a mist of water and chalk before performing on bars. This is a technique used to keep the grips from being too smooth and slippery. Grip brushes can also be used for the same purpose.

There is a vast amount of pressure and weight placed on the wrists of competitive gymnasts that can increase risk for injury. Quick jerking and rotating movements of the hands and wrists with the weight of their entire body forced down on a bent wrist adds great injury potential, including fractures, sprains and dislocations. For this reason, some gymnasts wear wrist supports during practice, and even while competing. While typically worn for vaulting, due to the number of pounding repetitions associated with the round-off entry to the vault, if an athlete is experiencing wrist weakness or soreness, wrist guards may also be utilized with other event training.

Wrist supports provide protection to the wrist while it is in a straight position and relieves pressure on the nerves, tendons and ligaments reducing pain and preventing injury from overuse. As with grips, wrist supports come in many brands, styles and sizes. Coaches usually recommend their favorite, but comfort is the main goal. Wrist supports range from $50-$75. Price cuts can be found if ordered in bulk so purchasing supports for the whole team might save some significant money.

Wrist supports last much longer than grips but, as with most gymnastics equipment, can get pretty smelly, and that's putting it mildly. Terry cloth wrist guards can be washed in the washing machine. Most wrist supports must be hand washed with a mild soap.

LEOTARDS

Considering it is really about a one-yard piece of material, it is hard to believe how much money we have invested in "leos" over the years. However, Jordyn spends more time in a leo than any other type of clothing.

The beginning of our leo-buying years was fun and easy. Jordyn loved any leo, no matter the pattern, style or price. As time went on, she became more and more specific and picky and now even thinks she would like to design a leotard.

The price of a leo can range from $15 to $300, depending on the style, the amount of bling and the brand. Practice leotards are typically sleeveless and cheaper while competition leos are long-sleeved, sparkled and more expensive. A team warm-up suit can add up to $200 to the total price of the competition apparel but are often worn for more than one season.

A growth spurt, however, can sometimes cause issues in the second season of wearing a competition leo. At one Level 6 meet when Jordyn was 8 years old, she saluted to the judges on bars, and then proceeded to pick her "leo wedgy". The judges deducted a tenth of a point from her score, which caused her coaches to file a dispute. The end result was a 0.05 deduction and a little lesson learned. Only pick your "leo wedgy" before you salute the judges or it becomes part of your routine.

A few years ago, I was given two giant shopping bags full of hand-me-down leos from a friend. Many of them did not pass Jordyn's comfort inspection. Having 20 or 30 unused leos, plus the attire that Jordyn had outgrown, inspired me to start a leo sale program at our gym. This is a successful annual event. Moms place each leo to be sold in a plastic bag with a pre-printed information slip indicating their name, size and price listed, typically $5 or $10. The organizers of the sale collect the money and slips and later distribute them to the sellers. Unsold leos are then donated. This sale is a great way to purchase leos and other gymnast's attire at bargain prices.

Sharing leos is another way to keep cost and inventory down. When Jordyn was about 14 years old, her locker room friends at the gym began swapping leotards. They would place all their leos in a "clean" basket and then could pick any that they wanted to wear for the day. The basket of "dirty" leos would go home with a different gymnast each week for laundry.

The cost of leotards may seem expensive, but compared to the gear and uniform apparel of other sports such as figure skating, ice hockey and lacrosse the cost is pretty reasonable.

THE BUN

One of the most stressful aspects of being a gym mom may very well be the creation of the perfect hair bun for competition. I have vivid memories of redoing, tightening, and smoothing Jordyn's bun until it had the appearance of plastic mannequin hair. Jordyn was not satisfied until it was perfect. Once it was perfect, the spray-on glitter could be applied, the final touch for the young competitive gymnast.

After many years in the bun-era I could create a perfect bun in my sleep. There was a time when I struggled with the bun. Jordyn has gigantic, frizzy/curly hair that does not like to be tamed. Her hair was a struggle to get in the hair tie without losing control of the tightness. Ironically, after secretly watching a dad do his daughter's bun one day in the gym, I perfected my technique and am proud to say Jordyn's bun rocked.

EASY STEPS TO THE PERFECT BUN

1) Spray the hair with a water bottle so that it is damp but not dripping wet.

2) Place a moderate amount of hair gel on the damp hair.

3) Using a fine-tooth comb, comb all the hair back into a ponytail. This may require 20 to 30 comb-backs of the hair to be sure every piece is perfectly smooth and flat.

4) Once the ponytail is in place, shellac it down with more hair gel and then spray generously with a strong-hold (preferably cheap) hairspray.

5) Now braid the ponytail. Jordyn's hair was so thick that I would need to split the ponytail into two or three small braids. Use small, thin rubber bands to hold the braids.

6) Take the braids (one at a time) and wrap them around the base of the ponytail tightly using many, many hairpins. The goal is for the braids to be immovably wrapped and secured around the base of the ponytail.

7) Spray the pinned braids with hairspray for good measure.

8) Place a bun cover around the secured braids. Then, apply the appropriate hair tie.

9) Finally, if desired, spray the entire head with glitter. Be sure to put a towel around your gymnast's shoulders to prevent glitter from getting all over her clothing.

the new life

Jordyn began competing as a gymnast when she was 7 years old and in second grade. Our oldest daughter, Lindsay, was 16; our son, Ryan, was 9 and our youngest, Kyra, was only 4. It is safe to say that Kyra does not really remember life without Jordyn being in gymnastics. Those early years were the busiest and hardest. Lindsay was able to drive, but we still did not want to miss any of her school activities. Ryan was at the peak of his extracurricular activities with piano lessons, basketball, soccer and flag football. Kyra was dancing and had recreational gymnastics. It was impossible for Dave and me to be four places at once, so the dividing of the family for most events became our norm.

CARPOOLS

I'm not going to lie, the minute I was able to ditch the family van, I did. I now have a tiny car that barely fits four people. The carpool era for the Wieber family is actually still in effect with our youngest child, but the carpools for four kids almost required a personal secretary and spreadsheet. Remember, carpools do not always go smoothly. One night, almost home from our 25-minute drive from the gym, my cell phone rang. I forgot one of the boys from our carpool. He was at the gym looking for me and finally called his mom. Fortunately, the mom was laid back and nice about the situation. She was fine with going to get him herself.

Jordyn was, and still is, very punctual. She must get to the gym on time, preferably early. There were numerous times when she would start to panic and even get teary-eyed if her ride was not on time.

Now that Jordyn can drive, life is much easier. We still participate

TIPS FOR GYMNASTICS TRAVELING

1. Use a checklist for packing gymnastics equipment.
   - Grips– two pairs
   - Wrist guards
   - Competition and warm-up leo
   - Warm-up suit
   - Footwear for the meet
   - Two copies of floor music (for optional gymnasts)
   - Athletic tape and pre-wrap
   - Hair ties, bobby pins, hairspray, spray glitter, scrunchies

2. If traveling by plane, carry on anything used for competition.

3. Get good directions or use a GPS to be sure you know how to get to the meet.

4. Avoid traveling on the day of competition if the drive is more than three or four hours.

5. Arrive at a meet at least 30 minutes before check-in.

in our carpool one night a week. The rest of the time, we just worry about Jordyn driving herself. That will never end.

TRAVELING FOR COMPETITION

In the early years of competition, most meets are within reasonable driving distance. Early starting meets might require an overnight at a hotel. Between carpools and sharing rooms with another mother and gymnast, the cost of traveling is typically not overwhelming.

As a gymnast progresses to the optional levels, teams typically travel out of state for competitive meets because there are fewer gymnasts competing per level in a given state. A couple times a year, depending on the club's competitive schedule, this may require a plane ride to a meet and more than one night in a hotel. Expenses can add up in a hurry.

At our gym, the competitions that required a flight were designated as "team trips" meaning the athletes would stay with each other and an adult chaperone. The small group of gymnasts would cover the travel cost of the chaperone. This helped the parents attend if finances may have prohibited them from traveling otherwise.

I tried hard to attend as many sporting events as possible for all of my children regardless of location. Since expenses can add up, sharing hotel rooms and using frequent flyer miles helped make it work. As Jordyn traveled farther and out of the country, my husband often stayed home to take care for the other kids. Jordyn understood and was happy that one of us could attend.

Probably the biggest impact Jordyn's gymnastics life had on our family was the dynamic of our vacations and weekends. Often times, either my husband or I would stay home with Jordyn while the rest of the family went on vacation or to the cottage. One year, we flew Jordyn and my older daughter, Lindsay, home early from a family vacation because it was all the time they could take off. Many of our friends and family members did not understand

6. For longer trips, plan on picking up healthy snacks for the hotel room rather than needing to hit the vending machines for a late night snack.

7. Avoid swimming in hotel pools before competition to prevent hands from becoming soft and rip easily on bars.

8. Enforce a curfew for bedtime at hotel stays the night before a meet. There is plenty of time for hotel fun after the competition.

9. Only share hotel rooms with those who have compatible habits as you and your gymnast.

10. Bring along something for your gymnast to eat for breakfast if you have an early meet. It's not the time to try something different or skip a meal.

11. Pack "just in case" items including safety pins, tape, hair ties, a sewing kit, spot remover, pain reliever, and the like.

how we could split up our family. To be honest, I often felt uneasy about the choices we made in the early years. I was torn between wanting to allow Jordyn every opportunity to progress in gymnastics and maintaining some sense of family normalcy for the other children.

While Jordyn was a Level 5, we still vacationed together but gymnastics remained a priority, especially in my mind. Once while on spring break in Florida, I drove her to two different gyms in Orlando so Jordyn could train. It was clearly my competitive nature more than Jordyn's that prompted me to do this, as her coach did not mandate it. She had to compete in a meet the day after we returned home, and I couldn't stand the thought of her doing poorly because she just been on vacation. Looking back now, I would consider this to be the beginning of my addiction to Jordyn's gymnastics.

We did not allow Jordyn to miss one meet and rarely a practice for the sake of a family vacation. Looking back, it was Level 5 for crying out loud. She had more than a dozen meets that year. Even at that early stage in the game, Jordyn did not want to miss the chance to compete, and I did not want to see her miss. It is easy to think I was going overboard, but I am not sure I would do anything differently if I had it to do over again. Jordyn also did not want to miss practice or meets either. I was not forcing her to forgo fun. It was her choice as well. That intensity in Jordyn's personality has always helped me rationalize some of my own behavior.

SCHOOL AND SPORTS

There are 168 hours in a week. Subtract from that nine-hours of sleep each night for a growing adolescent and that leaves 105 hours of awake time. Then subtract seven hours of school for five of those days, and you are down to 70 hours. Subtract from that 23 hours of gymnastics practice, which is about average for a competitive gymnast and you are left with 47 hours of free time per week, or about 6-and-a-half hours each day. After fitting in time for personal hygiene, eating, and homework there's not much time for a social life in the day of a gymnast. That is probably why the club becomes the main social arena for competitive gymnasts. It always amazes me when I hear of other gymnasts who still engage in school sports, such as cheerleading, diving, soccer, dance and more.

Since kindergarten, Jordyn has not participated in any other sport besides gymnastics. In fact, once she started on the elite path, around age 9, to prevent possible injury, she did not participate in gym class. At our request, the school allowed her credit for gym class from her gymnastics participation. Once again, looking back that does sound quite extreme, but at the time, she was moving on the fast track and she did not want anything to get in the way.

Jordyn (3ʳᵈ grade) and her brother, Ryan (4ᵗʰ grade) on the first day of school.

In addition to gym class, the school day had to be negotiated when Jordyn was in third grade. At this point, she was placed in a training group that started at 3:30 p.m. rather than 4:30 p.m. Her school was not dismissed until 3:45 p.m. so she had to leave school about an hour early everyday. I remember feeling awkward talking to the principal about Jordyn's need to leave early. I felt like he thought I was one of those overly competitive moms who thought her kid was the best at their sport. He went on to tell me that there were lots of kids who did club sports that required extra practice. He couldn't allow one to be off school and not everyone. Granted, at this point Jordyn was 9 years old and was competing at Level 8, along with a few other Level 8 gymnasts from our school district. She was on the fast track but had not established any real notoriety in the local, non-gymnastics setting. It was finally decided that the principal would put Jordyn in gym class the last period of the day. It was a great compromise since I did not really want her participating in gym anyway.

Most every competitive gymnast comes to a point in the season where they must miss a few days of school to travel to a meet. It was, of course, Jordyn's responsibility to keep up with her schoolwork. She eventually became very comfortable at informing her teachers a few days in advance of her absence to get any work she might miss.

The real struggle for Jordyn began in fifth grade when she started morning workouts three-days a week. At this point, Jordyn qualified as an international elite gymnast, so we had a bit more justification behind our request. The school district was very flexible in putting Jordyn with teachers who understood her situation and would provide her with missed assignments. Despite our negotiated absences, I received a form letter from the school counselor that addressed her school absences. The letter said something like, "It seems you may be having difficulty getting your child to school on time, and we'd like to help." There was a list of options for accepting their help, including, "We are willing to come to your home and help get your daughter to school each morning, if you are unable to do so."

I'm pretty sure the counselor did not realize our situation with gymnastics, but I almost took them up on that offer with my other kids just to make my life easy. Hey, as long as they were offering!

When Jordyn reached high school it became impossible for her to miss three mornings of school each week and still keep up. We are fortunate that our state has a program called Michigan Virtual High School that provides online classes but utilizes the public school as the "mentor." She began taking two classes online and only going to school in the afternoons for the other two classes. All grades are reported to our high school and show up on Jordyn's transcript. She attends public school in the afternoons and will still graduate as usual with her class in 2013.

Some of the gymnasts at Twistars are homeschooled. Some of Jordyn's friends on the U.S. National Team are also homeschooled. Since we had the opportunity to coordinate Jordyn's schedule and keep her in public schools, that is the choice we made.

As a former schoolteacher, I personally felt strongly that I did not want Jordyn to miss out on the experience of attending high school. Jordyn loves going to lunch with her school friends every day. She socializes with her school friends whenever she can by going to movies, games and dances. If we had a greater travel distance to the gym, a school district that would not cooperate with us, or no option for partial online schooling, we very well could have opted for homeschooling.

We feel fortunate that we were able to keep Jordyn's life balanced in such a way, though it has not always been easy. She is typically behind when she returns from training camps or meets and works diligently to catch up.

IMPACT ON SIBLINGS

I learned a long time ago, well before our life in gymnastics, that things are not always even or fair. Sometimes, one child requires more time than another. Sometimes, one child's sport costs more than another. With the age-span of our children, there was no way to keep things even. There was a time when I was attending kindergarten graduation for Kyra one week, then going to Lindsay's high school graduation the next. It might be easier for some families to keep things evenly divided and distributed. In our family, it was not possible. Despite our goals of teaching our children that they are all equally important to us and everything that they accomplish is wonderful, there were times when things became very out-of-balance, and we heard about it. In general, our kids are very supportive of each other. Sibling rivalry does not really come into play, mostly because of the age-spacing and gender differences. Ryan, our quarterback football player, never felt like he was not good enough despite the fact that his sister won the World Championships in the middle of his senior year

The Wieber siblings: Lindsay, Jordyn, Ryan and Kyra in 2003.

football season. Our older daughter had gone to college before the youngest even began playing sports. We happily avoided the sibling rivalry storm.

The touchy situations usually stemmed from Jordyn getting lots of "stuff." We did provide Jordyn with incentives for her hard work and performance. When she earned an iPhone for winning the AT&T American Cup one year, you can imagine the other kids thinking that was quite unfair. We tried to explain to the kids our rationale that Jordyn has made many sacrifices in her life to be at her level. She cannot ski each weekend in the winter with the others. She has missed several family vacations over spring break. She can rarely do sleepovers with her friends because of early morning workouts all summer and on Saturdays. This was our way of providing her with rewards.

Yet to be quite honest, we probably did spoil all of our kids a bit too much in an effort to keep things somewhat in balance. Kyra did not get an iPhone, but we did give her Jordyn's old phone when she was only 9 years old. This was something I probably would not have done otherwise.

I am sure there were times when the other kids were not thrilled that only one of their parents came to their games because the other was with Jordyn at a gymnastics meet. On the other hand, I have missed plenty of concerts and sporting events because of my 12-hour work schedule. So, kids need to know about real life. We have tried to consider the whole situation "teachable." They have learned how to be flexible and that every situation has a solution. Not bad life lessons.

CHAPTER FOUR
coaches

Jordyn and her coach, John Geddert, in the early years.

During the past 24 years, my children participated in dance, piano, soccer, flag football, tackle football, soccer, swimming, lacrosse, basketball, wrestling, track and field, volleyball, and, of course, gymnastics. I have worked with parent coaches, student coaches, teacher coaches, and career coaches. I have been the spouse of a coach, the mother of a coach and even coached myself. One common thread I have found in all these situations is that coaches care about kids. There is not enough money in coaching for someone to take on such a time-consuming role solely for financial gain.

I have seen coaches act poorly, yell, degrade athletes, treat athletes unfairly, lie and even cheat. Caring about kids does not always equate to being a great coach. Coaching is not easy. It takes an inordinate amount of time, patience, skill, kindness, tough love and finesse.

the great gymnastics coach

What really makes a great gymnastics coach? The answer is both objective and subjective. A parent can look at statistics as a way of measuring the greatness of a coach. How many state, regional and national champions were coached? How many athletic scholarships were earned?

A parent can also look at experience and knowledge. A coach with many years of experience has surely learned a thing or two. Newer coaches have yet to acquire such wisdom but may be savvy to newer techniques and are definitely closer in age to the gymnasts, which can be either a plus or a minus.

A coach cannot be great without athletes who will work with them. A gymnast cannot be great without a coach who helps her reach her

highest potential. A harmoni-
ous gymnast/coach fit is key in
finding a great coach for your
daughter. If the coach and
gymnast do not connect with
each other, or the coach's style
does not work for the athlete,
the athlete's full potential may
never be reached. A coach's

Jordyn and coach, Kathryn Geddert.

style that works wonders for one athlete may not work for another.

In every instance, the coach and the gymnast need each other to create greatness. If the gymnast does not want to train in the manner that the coach requires, the relationship is not going to work. If the coach can't mentally connect with the gymnast, it won't work. It is a two way street.

A common question since Jordyn's recent success is why we stayed at our gym in Michigan when there were many other, more established elite gyms and coaches. The reason was simple. John and Kathryn's coaching styles, their instruction of technical moves and corrections make sense to Jordyn. There is an incredible fit, and it works.

the long and winding road

Using an average of 25 hours of practice per week over the past 12 years, Jordyn has spent more than 15,000 hours with her gymnastics coaches. I'd be lying if I said all of those hours were perfect. She had her moments of frustration and tears. She has been sent to climb the rope and to the locker room for a time out. We have had private meetings once or twice a year with her coaches to be sure we are on the same page with goals, expectations and plans.

The relationship between a coach and athlete is very special. It would almost be unusual if emotions did not become overwhelming in some circumstances. That does not mean, however, that the relationship is not working. It is natural for ups and downs to occur in any situation where two people are working together so hard for so many hours.

How do you know, then, if the coach/athlete relationship is working or not? Ask yourself these questions:

- Is my daughter progressing in the sport?
- Does my daughter look forward to going to practice?
- Does my daughter respect her coach?
- Do I feel comfortable communicating with the coach?
- Do I feel my daughter is receiving adequate attention?

If the answer is "no" to any of the above questions, there might not be the best coach/athlete/parent fit. The relationship between the coach and parent can be as important as the one between the coach and gymnast. Everyone needs to be happy and content.

COMMUNICATING WITH COACHES

As with parents, friends, family and teachers, anyone who spends such a significant amount of time with your child plays a major role in her development and life.

Having a comfortable, open relationship with your daughter's coach is crucial. You should feel like the door is always open for discussions or question. Keep in mind that while your daughter has one coach, that coach has many athletes. The coach's time is valuable and limited. Frequent texting, emailing, calling or stopping the coach in the gym for trivial questions or comments only takes time away from the athletes.

So how do you know when and how to communicate with your daughter's coach? Here are a few tips for establishing effective and appropriate communication with the coach.

- Upon joining the gym, ask the coach how he or she prefers to communicate with you.

- If there is not an established annual parent-coach conference scheduled at your gym, request one. Consider it to be like a parent-teacher conference. The end of a competitive season is a great time to sit down for 15 or 20 minutes with the coach to review the previous season and discuss goals and plans for the next. Knowing you have that conference pre-established, keep track of questions you come up with throughout the season and take the list to the meeting.

- If you have a concern, be sure to talk to your daughter first to see how she perceives the situation. I have caught myself being very upset and irritated about situations that did not phase Jordyn. If the situation concerns you and your daughter, consider asking for a meeting with the coach that includes your child. It is important for your daughter to see you communicate effectively and maturely with her coach so she realizes everyone has her best interest at heart.

DIFFICULT COACHES

While coaches who engage in verbal abuse and excessive punishment are rare, this is still a topic that should legitimately be addressed in a chapter about coaches.

THE SHARP TONGUE

There is a fine line between verbal use and verbal abuse to motivate an athlete. We have all seen movies and television shows with coaches "inspiring" their athletes by telling them how pathetic they looked out on the field or that they are "sissies" or other words inappropriate for this book. In my mind, this attempt at motivation could be effective in a team setting that is not directed at individual players.

Verbal bullying not only rarely works, but also can destroy a child's self-esteem and love of the sport. There may be the occasional athlete who wants to prove the coach wrong and will work harder and perform better more often.

Bullying is not always in the form of verbal abuse. Hand gestures, body language, facial expression and even lack of attention can have equally destructive effects on an athlete. While the occasional use of such actions can be effective, regular, purposeful gestures by a coach communicate to an athlete that she is worthless and can be devastating.

As a mother, I do not tolerate this behavior. It would not matter if she was training with the greatest coach ever, no one will bully my child. So what do parents do if they suspect this conduct from their daughter's coach? First, calm down, then organize your thoughts and concerns and schedule a private meeting with the coach. It is important to get both sides of the story. The other side of the story may, in fact, include your own child being disrespectful or lying to the coach or even cheating on training requirements. Not that this warrants verbal abuse and name calling, but that information may be useful in developing an action plan for dealing with the situation.

EXCESSIVE PUNISHMENT

A coach's job is to get the most out of the athlete. Sometimes, this requires negative reinforcement. Requiring athletes to do extra work, such as push-ups or running laps in response to poor performance, is not a new concept. Making an athlete sit on the bench is another effective strategy that may elicit a greater effort in the long run. Gymnastics is no different than any other sport in that most coaches will not tolerate a weak effort or laziness. Adding extra conditioning or more repetitions to routines or having a gymnast take a break in the locker room should not be considered excessive punishment.

However, if a coach's negative reinforcement techniques go beyond what you would consider appropriate, as the parent and advocate for your child, you may need to step in. In a sport that already requires many hours of training, requiring extra conditioning or repetitions that leave the gymnast overly sore or even injured is inappropriate.

Once again, the rule of thumb is to communicate your concerns to the coach in a private setting. I have seen and heard of many situations where parents were unhappy about the punitive treatment their athlete received yet would not address concerns and speak with the coach. A parent should not be afraid of repercussions from speaking to a coach. Remember, the parent is paying for a service and it is appropriate to discuss concerns.

let the coach coach

My oldest daughter, Lindsay, excelled at track and field in her early years. I was a collegiate scholarship athlete in track and field, and this was my area of passion and expertise. I took on the role of Lindsay's coach before she was old enough to be on a track team because there was no other option. There was no track club or coach in our area for someone in her circumstance.

Once Lindsay began organized track and field in junior high school, I surrendered my coaching duties to her new coaches. This was very hard for me. I was a long jumper for eight years. To sit and watch Lindsay be coached by someone else in an event that I knew everything about was very difficult. Now and then, I would try to sneak in coaching suggestions to Lindsay at home, even though I knew it was not in her best interest.

On the other hand, my experience in gymnastics was nothing more than one year on the high school gymnastics team where I performed a squat-over on the vault and earned a score of 4.600. After spending that entire season trying to learn a back handspring with no success, I knew my career wasn't going to take off. I know nothing about gymnastics. It has always been easy for me to let the coaches do their thing. Based on my observations and conversations with many gym moms, I have learned that this is not so easy for everyone.

The bottom line is you are paying good money for a coach to coach your daughter. Let them do their job! Even Olympic gold medalist Mary Lou Retton, now the mother of three competitive gymnasts, says she lets the coaches do their job and rarely watches practice (see interview with Mary Lou Retton in Chapter 5).

Your daughter's coach has a specific plan for training, skill progression and routine development. For coaches, taking the time to listen to a parent's suggestions for routines or training is not only a waste of their time but also frustrating. While coaches have told me they welcome useful information about their athletes that may be relevant for program development, constant critiquing and recommendations from parents are a different story.

the bottom line

The parent is the gymnast's biggest advocate. The parent is ultimately responsible for the child's well-being. Be sure to be comfortable and happy with your daughter's coach. Your daughter deserves the best chance to reach her highest potential in the sport of gymnastics. In summary, choose your gym and coaches carefully. Keep open communication with the coach and your daughter. Sit back and let the coaches coach.

CHAPTER FIVE
the parent

Jordyn and her "Gym Mom".

very parent wants their children to be successful and to provide them with all the tools needed to flourish in life. We want them to have the edge, to be competitive, to win. The road to success starts, according to some, even in the prenatal years. There are actual educational programs designed for fetuses in the womb. No wonder my son doesn't like to read, he didn't start looking at books until he was the ripe old age of 6 months! I clearly should have been reading to him as a fetus.

Just as we want our children to have an intellectual edge, the path to athletic triumph can begin at a very young age. There is a growing trend of developmental programs designed to expose children to organized sports as early as age 3. Many sports programs have year-round options for those who specialize in their area of athletic prowess.

As with any sport, the competitive nature of parents becomes evident in the world of gymnastics and that's not necessarily a bad thing. We live in a competitive world. Gymnastics, and almost all sports, imparts lessons of determination, teamwork and drive. Success and winning are what drives athletes. That feeling of training hard and accomplishing a goal is like no other. Success feels great. Winning is fun.

What is concerning, however, is when the competitive nature of parents exposes itself in a less than appealing manner. I've seen it. I've done it. It's very easy to get carried away and consumed by a sport. Especially one in which your daughter excels.

Looking back at the last 10 years of Jordyn's competitive career, I think I was more consumed with her performance in the early years. As an athlete myself, I have a competitive nature. Put me in a group of other competitive parents with a daughter who has talent, and I bordered on the inappropriate side more than a few times.

I remember spending hours pouring over charts of TOPs testing cut off scores, averages and records from previous years to predict how

Jordyn ranked. At one TOPs testing session parent viewing was not allowed. There was, however, a large garage door to the building that was raised about 12 inches. Many of the moms, including me, lay on the ground to peek through the opening, trying to get a glimpse of our daughters' performances. I'm sure that must have looked ridiculous to anyone passing by.

the competitive gym mom

Not every mother of a gymnast should be categorized as a "competitive gym mom." I am a soccer mom and a football mom, and in neither of those situations do I believe I am as "competitive" as I am in my role as a gym mom. In those situations, I am more relaxed, don't need to know about each and every practice, and rarely communicate with the coach. Sure, I want to see my child succeed, but I don't see myself as having a major role in that success as I feel I do as a gym mom. It may be the individual aspect of gymnastics or even the intensity of the sport; regardless, my behavior differs as a parent of a gymnast than it does as a soccer or football mom.

My philosophy is that parent behavior manifests itself from a desire for control. To relinquish control of a major chunk of your child's life is difficult. Whether or not the extreme conduct makes a difference in your child's performance or success doesn't really matter. It's the feeling that you have some control over the situation that allows for a certain degree of coping.

WATCHING PRACTICE

When Jordyn had her first three-hour gymnastics practice, I really didn't know what to do with myself. My husband and I had not experienced a child attending a sports practice for more than an hour and a half. With a 2 year old along for the ride, staying to watch practice was not a good option for me. I never really got into the habit of staying to watch long practices. Fortunately, this was fine with Jordyn. Even as a very young gymnast, she really did not care one-way or the other if I watched. I would, however, try to watch an hour or two every now and then, so Jordyn could show me her new skills.

Like many gyms, ours has an upstairs viewing area. It is not uncommon to see a line up of moms (and dads) watching practice for four or five hours. I am sure most coaches do not have a problem with that unless it becomes distracting to the gymnast. It is important for parents to have a good sense of the gym environment and how their daughter is doing at practice. I am not a fan of closed-gyms or those that do not allow viewing. Yet, through the years, I have seen and heard of a few situations where the parent watching became a bit over-the-top.

COACHING FROM THE VIEWING AREA

In my many interviews conducted with coaches, I have never had one of them say they appreciate it when parents hand-gesture or mouth instructions to their gymnasts from the viewing area. Trying to tell the gymnast, for example, to point toes, keep legs straight, or get more height is not only distracting but also somewhat disrespectful to the coach. Some kids do need constant approval from their parents and, therefore, may look to them for signals during practice. When parents provide approval or disapproval to their child during practice, it can become something that the gymnast expects when she should be looking to her coach for feedback.

As hard as it might be, a parent who has the tendency to coach from the bench should think about spending a little less time in the gym.

TRACKING THE COACH'S TIME

It's easy to get caught up in comparisons in a sport such as gymnastics. That is one of the many reasons I have not made it a habit to watch long practices often. In my more competitive years, I would catch myself noticing if the coach was spending more or less time with Jordyn compared to other athletes. When Jordyn seemed to be getting more attention I felt a little guilty. When she seemed to be getting less direct attention, I would get irritated. It was better for me not to watch.

I have realized through my conversations with many coaches, that their main concern is helping each gymnast reach her next goal. If the next goal is to remain consistent through the season and polish skills, that requires less direct coaching time than another gymnast who is trying to acquire a new skill. One day, one child might get more coaching time, and the next, it might be someone else. My best advice is to trust the coach. As long as your child is happy and progressing, things are good. It was an important lesson for me.

COMPARING GYMNASTS

As a collegiate long jumper, I learned a valuable, yet painful lesson about competition -- what happens on competition day is what counts. In 1985, the qualifying distance to go to the NCAA Championships in the long jump was 20 feet, 1 inch. In practice, I jumped further on two occasions. During an actual competition, however, the furthest I could accomplish was 19 feet, 9 inches. Unfortunately, what I did during practice was not official and I never qualified for the NCAA Champion-ships. Even though my jump of 19 feet 9 inches would have medaled that year in the NCAA Championships, it did not matter. I was not there.

The same lesson holds true with all sports, including gymnastics. It does not make sense to compare scores from one gymnast to another. If they are competing against each other on a given day, a winner will be determined. I still catch myself, 30 years after college, comparing my times and distances in track and field to achievements of current athletes. It's silly. The same holds true with comparing gymnastics scores from year to year, or even meet to meet. The outcome of a competition on a given day, even if it's by an outrageously slim margin, determines the winner, regardless of past statistics, trends, odds, or records. That's what makes competition exciting.

REWARDS, PUNISHMENTS AND INCENTIVES

Probably one of the most controversial topics in youth sports is parental punishment for poor performance. While I cannot fathom such conduct, I have heard stories that make my skin crawl. It's hurtful to punish the gymnast if things don't work out the way the parent imagined.

Rewards and incentives, on the other hand, can play a role in youth sports, especially gymnastics. My philosophy stems from the fact that most adults respond to rewards and incentives. We work for paychecks. We work harder for bonus pay. Rewards and incentives motivate people. Sure, it is great to feel fulfilled and satisfied for a job well done, but the bonuses or added incentives make life a little more fun.

The sport of gymnastics requires hours and hours of training all year

SAMPLE INCENTIVE CHART FOR JORDYN—LEVEL 8

ACHIEVEMENT	REWARD
9.0 on any event	iTunes download
9.5 or higher on any event	$5.00
Qualifying to regionals	CD
No falls (four for four)	stuffed animal
36.0 All-around score	$10
37.0 All-around score	$20
First Place All-Around	Movie date with a friend

long with very few days off. The rewards that come with competition are only available a few times a year. In elite gymnastics, it is not unusual for an athlete to compete only three or four times a year. That is a lot of hard work for a few chances at recognition.

I have always provided incentives and rewards to Jordyn for her hard work. Deep inside, I realize this was another attempt to control Jordyn's performance, something of which I had no control. To be honest, I think I thought Jordyn would actually try harder with an added reward attached to her performance. Now, looking back, I realize that probably was not the case. When Jordyn was a young Silverstars team member, part of the accelerated group of gymnasts, she would train for 18 months before her first competition. Compared to other youth sports, such as basketball or soccer with weekly games, that was an extremely long time to work at something without the opportunity to show your skill. At that time, I instituted an incentive program that would reward Jordyn for mastering new skills. Once she learned a new skill and could do it consistently, she would get a reward. Some of my gym mom friends considered this bribery. I did not. Jordyn still had a feeling of pride and fulfillment when she learned a new skill. My contribution was an extra reward for her hard work.

Once Jordyn started competing, we worked together to create an incentive chart each season. Rewards were not just based on winning but also for attaining personal goals. During her younger years rewards were often toys.

As she got older, we started rewarding her with money – typically in the form of a "line of credit." This meant that I kept a tab of what Jordyn earned. I functioned as her bank. When she wanted to purchase something special, I would buy it for her and subtract it from her line of credit. As a young teenager, due to her busy schedule, she didn't have the opportunity to earn money in conventional ways, such as babysitting. She was required to do chores at home, but we never established an allowance for our children, rather just expected them to help. We did pay our children for doing larger chores or projects at home, but again, Jordyn didn't have much spare time. Her gymnastics incentives became her source of income. We kept the incentive program going until Jordyn was about 15 years old. At that point, she told us she didn't want to do it anymore.

Despite losing that sense of power and influence I felt by offering Jordyn the rewards, I was actually relieved when she didn't want them anymore. If there was ever a time that I felt as though I was going overboard, it was with the rewards. What started as small trinkets and privileges became ridiculous big-ticket items that she really didn't need. Those items were always offered by me as a last ditch effort to think I was doing something that would actually affect her performance. It was crazy, and I knew it. I felt like a hypocrite in a way. One minute, I would tell my husband stories of overly competitive moms that I observed at a meet, and the next, I would throw out a huge incentive in an effort to impact Jordyn's outcome.

Thankfully, life is about learning and growing. I still believe in providing incentives, but not to the extent that had evolved. As with most things in life, moderation is often the key.

being involved

Opportunities to be part of your child's gymnastics life exist just as they do in school, church or with other sports. Many gymnastics clubs are

WHAT GYMNASTS AND GYM MOMS SAID ABOUT REWARDS AND PUNISHMENTS

Q: Are/were you ever punished for not competing or training well? How?

A: I was given the silent treatment at meets on occasion for not performing up to my full potential. That was always hard as I never felt like I was competing badly on purpose. I feel like sometimes they added to my own disappointment.

We were often yelled at during practice to work hard or fix form, but I don't feel we were necessarily punished. The worst thing I can remember is being videotaped and then shown our practice to show how poorly we were working out. It was hard as we were compared to the younger girls who always seemed to be "favored" over the older generation.

Former Level 8 gymnast

A: Ever since I was little I was always told that gymnastics is for me and only me. It was not to impress anyone else, only for me to do the best I could, have fun and be proud of my accomplishments. I took this to heart. The only person that ever got upset with me after not competing or training well was me, and it taught me a lot of self discipline. When my parents or coaches could tell I was upset they always told me that it was ok and that I just had to work harder to get better so I would be happy. I have always been my biggest critic and pushed my self much harder than anyone else could, even outside of gymnastics. I think this has helped me succeed in so many things I have done.

Gigja, former gymnast

A: Thankfully I had two awesome parents who understood how grueling the training and competition at the highest level can be. If I had a good attitude and was giving 100% I never got punished for not competing or training well. It was the times where I'd give my coach the "teenage attitude" and not give the effort that I was fully capable of giving that I would get in a lot of trouble. The way my parents and coach would punish me was to sit me down and have a brutally honest conversation. They would tell me that whatever I choose to do in life, it was imperative that I gave it 100%. If I wasn't going to give it my all, then it was a waste of time for me and

continued...

...a waste of time for them.

I can only remember a few times where I got rewarded for doing well. I vividly remember when I was 10 years old and learning my Tkatchev on bars. I had been easily catching it on the pit bar for a few weeks. From the outside looking in, there was nothing scary about it. My Tkatchev was very good, high flying and had very nice form. One day, for no reason, I decided that I wasn't going to do it anymore because I was scared. My coach told me that if I caught one on the next turn she would give me $100. Being the competitor I am, I got up and not only caught one, but did three in one turn while I was on the bar. Talk about being a little sucker on my part. Looking back I would be annoyed with me, too! My coach was prepared to give me the $100, but when my mother found out... boy, was I in TROUBLE. She wasn't upset because I had been scared of my Tkatchev; she was upset with the fact that when bribed with $100, I could do it with no problem. By my behavior and how I responded to the situation, it was clear that I didn't have a real fear of the skill. I just didn't have enough discipline to make myself go for the skill every time to get past my fears. My mother told my coach that I was absolutely not allowed to receive the $100. Instead I got to pick out a free leotard from the gym's selection. As a 10 year old, I was still thrilled to get a free leotard from my shenanigans, but was fully aware to never let something like that happen again! Being in trouble wasn't worth it.

Tasha Schwikert, 2000 Olympic bronze medalist

A: Sometimes, we reward her for achieving goals that she has worked extremely hard for. We feel it's important to set goals in life. A reward for achieving those goals helps to stay focused and motivated. Gabrielle sets her goals and then we agree on a reward based on her recommendation. The reward has ranged from a sleepover, to ice cream, to a new pair of shoes. At one point she was begging for a cell phone and it happened to be at a time when she was struggling in gymnastics. She asked if she could get a cell phone if she accomplished her goals. These were pretty extreme goals that she set, so we agreed. She reached her goals and we said, "Let's go pick out your new phone." My daughter said that she no longer wanted a phone because she felt she still could have done even better. She is a great goal setter, and she is her toughest critic.

Tanya Toonen, Gym mom

full of moms who are employed in the gym office or as recreational coaches. Many former gymnasts-now-gym moms enjoy being in a familiar environment that fulfills them.

When Jordyn began gymnastics at age 4, I had a newborn baby. Staying at the gym, in any capacity, was not possible for me at that time. I did, however, fulfill our Booster Club's required responsibilities, which were to be part of one standing committee for the year and to volunteer at our annual fundraiser gymnastics meet. This was more than enough for me at the time. As the years progressed, I became more involved in effort to do my part for the gym and Booster Club.

BOOSTER CLUB INVOLVEMENT

Booster clubs are not unique to gymnastics. They are formed by any group of enthusiasts (often parents) to provide support, usually financial, to a sports team or club. Not every gymnastics club has a booster club. The creation of a booster club requires a group of dedicated parents working closely with the club owners and following all of the rules and regulations that go with being a 501(c)(3) nonprofit organization. It can be a tricky situation in the gymnastics setting. The principle of the nonprofit is that the booster club cannot discriminate in providing benefits to the athletes based on their family's membership, time or fundraising efforts. All athletes must receive the same benefit from the booster club.

Gymnastics competition schedules and costs vary greatly based on the level of the gymnast.

In some non-profit organization the State mandates that dues collected must be the same for all families yet not all families receive the same benefit from the booster club. Dues often cover meet entry fees and coaching costs. Not all gymnasts compete in the same number of meets in a given year. An injured gymnast may not compete at all. It is difficult for families to justify the additional financial burden of booster club dues on top of gym fees with a gymnast, who cannot compete. The uniqueness of the sport of gymnastics can complicate the financial impetus of the club beyond what many want to manage.

The Booster Club at Twistars USA is considered by some to be one of the largest and most successful in the nation. Every competitive gymnast family, both boys and girls, in Level 5 and above must belong to the club.

The Booster Club is under the direction of a board of nine parents, whom are elected each year. Each member of the club pays monthly dues between $100 and $175 that help cover competitive entry fees, a week of summer camp at Twistars and more. Each family is required to be on one standing committee and work a designated number of hours, typically 20-24, at our annual invitational.

The operation of a Booster Club as large as the one at Twistars is equivalent to running a small business. When I had time in my life to become more involved at the gym, I jumped in pretty deep. After complaining about some of the operations of our current booster club, someone told me that if I did not like how things were, then I should get involved.

A few months later, I was elected the vice president of the club. As the vice president, the roll of Invitational Chair was included. Our annual invitational grew to more than 1,600 gymnasts competing in 12 gymnastics sessions for three days. Coordinating this event took hundreds of hours of my time. While I found the project to be rewarding, one year of such a monumental task was enough for me.

The next year I became the booster club president. One advantage of this position was the chance to make some changes that I thought would be beneficial. It was my goal to improve booster club communication to all members, put monthly meetings on a regular schedule and vary the day of the week to allow more members to attend. I looked at my role as president as a chance to be the voice of the entire membership and that made me feel useful. After two years on the board, I needed to volunteer time to my other children.

MAINTAINING BALANCE

The two years I was heavily involved in the booster club at our gym sometimes created an imbalance in our family. My husband and the other children were very aware that gymnastics was absorbing all of my free time. On top of the volunteer work, I still drove the gymnastics carpool and traveled to Jordyn's meets.

Even I could tell that gymnastics was beginning to consume me. My thoughts were on gymnastics almost every waking moment. If I wasn't working on something for the booster club or the invitational, I was surfing the web looking at gymnastics meet results. I was being sucked into this one aspect of my life and was gradually losing interest in anything else. By the end of the two years, I knew that I had to regain a healthier balance. I could still enjoy and support Jordyn's gymnastics career without being so consumed.

After my two involved years at the gym, I made a conscious effort to step back and let Jordyn pave her own way. If her life took a different direction than the dream I had for her, so be it. It is her life.

the bottom line

The gym mom I am today is much different than the gym mom I was 12 years ago. Part of the reason for writing this book is to share what I have learned through my experience. I'm not sure if it is through retrospect, or just the wisdom of being older, but I sure don't sweat the small stuff now like I did 10 or 20 years ago.

My youngest daughter, with five years of school sports still ahead, will no doubt have the benefit of a wiser, calmer, less "competitive" mom cheering with unconditional support in the stands. And in the end, that is really all our children want.

AN INTERVIEW WITH
MARY LOU RETTON

In preparation for this book, I had the honor of interviewing Mary Lou Retton. Mary Lou was the first American woman to ever win a gold medal in gymnastics when she won the all-around title at the 1984 Olympic Games in Los Angeles. She and her husband, Shannon Kelley, have 4 daughters, 3 of whom are competitive gymnasts. I asked Mary Lou about her life as both a former gymnast and a gym mom.

RITA What type of role did your mother play in your gymnastics career?

MARY LOU My mother was a very hands off parent for which I felt blessed. She was extremely support-   ive but never put unnecessary pressure on me.

RITA (Mary Lou left her family home at age 14 to train in Houston, Texas with Bela and Martha Karolyi) How did you and your mother handle your moving away to train with Bela?

Mary Lou Retton and Jordyn at the 2006 Visa Championships.

MARY LOU It was a difficult decision to make (letting your 14yr old daughter leave home) but she wanted me to go after my dream. The best shot of me making the Olympics was moving to Houston to train with Bela & Martha.

RITA As a young gymnast, did your parents offer you incentives for achieving goals? If so, do you feel that was a motivating factor for you?

MARY LOU No, I set my own goals.

RITA How was it becoming a "Gym Mom" after such a successful gymnastics career?

MARY LOU Very natural. I put my girls into gym because I love the sport not thinking I would have three competitive gymnasts. I just love it.

RITA How do you react when your daughters are competing?

MARY LOU Proud but nervous as well.

RITA Did you have any superstitions or rituals as a competitive gymnast? Do you find yourself with any superstitions or rituals when your daughters compete?

MARY LOU Yes, I did. I always put my right grip on first and if I performed bad or got injured in a certain leo, I never wore it again. I have no rituals when I watch my daughters.

RITA Do you watch your daughters train?

MARY LOU Rarely, I let their coaches do their jobs. If they have a big meet coming up I'll watch them a few days before we leave for the competition to see if they are prepared.

continued...

RITA. Do you provide coaching tips to your daughters or to their coaches?

MARY LOU. Only if they ask for it. My job is to be a supportive mom not a coach.

RITA. What advice would you give to the mother of a competitive gymnast based on your experience as a gymnast and a "Gym Mom?"

MARY LOU. To always be there with a listening ear, a shoulder to cry on and arms wide open for big bear hugs!!

RITA. Aside from being the first American to win the Olympic Gold and the life changing effect that had for you– what do you feel you gained the most from being a competitive gymnast?

MARY LOU. A terrific work ethic that I have carried with me through-out my adult life.

CHAPTER SIX
keeping your gymnast healthy

As the mother of a gymnast, Jordyn's health is the biggest source of stress and worry for me. It was much easier to control her lifestyle behaviors when she was younger. I could enforce a bedtime, cook her meals, and be sure she took her vitamins. Jordyn's emergence into her teenage years brought all the typical power struggles and rebellion that one would expect with any adolescent. Realistically, I knew that unless I kept her in a bubble, she would encounter germs like everyone else in the world. I did everything in my power to keep her immune system strong, but through the years, we had our share of untimely illnesses.

Once as I slept the night before a Level 5 meet, Jordyn came into my room saying she didn't feel good. She had a fever. The competitive side of me contemplated dosing her up with Tylenol, and having her compete anyway. The mom in me knew she needed to rest and get better. So she missed the meet, rested and got better.

Shortly after Jordyn became an elite gymnast, our club attended a meet in Texas where they had a separate elite division. This was the first time she was separated from her team as an elite gymnast in competition. I was looking forward to her chance to shine without having to compete against her Level 10 friends. This meet was designated as a "team trip" for our club, meaning that the gymnasts didn't stay with their own parents, but with a parent chaperone in separate rooms. Experiencing my usual pre-meet insomnia the night before Jordyn's competition, I didn't fall asleep until 2:00 a.m. About an hour later, my cell phone woke me up. Jordyn had thrown up all over the room, and in the bed, as well as on the way to the bathroom. I felt horrible for Jordyn, the chaperone and all the girls stuck in that room. The chaperone of the group asked me to run to the all-night store and get Jordyn some medicine.

I dragged myself out to the car and drove to the nearby store in a fog. I took the medicine to Jordyn and then I went back to bed.

The next morning, I realized that I probably should have taken Jordyn back to my room to spare the other athletes from getting sick. The girls ended up changing rooms for the remainder of the trip and I nursed Jordyn for three days while all of the other athletes competed.

the essentials

Whenever someone congratulates me on my daughter's accomplishments, I always mention that she is the one doing the hard work. I just make sure she stays fed, rested and gets to the gym on time. There is no secret to the care and feeding of a gymnast.

SLEEP

Of course, growing children require more sleep than adults. Typically, hard-working athletes have no problem wanting to go to sleep after a long, busy day. The problem usually comes with not having available hours to dedicate to sleep.

Jordyn has always appreciated her sleep time.

When Jordyn was in elementary school she practiced until 9 p.m. By the time she got home, ate dinner and got ready for bed, it was 10 p.m. at the earliest and that was without allowing time for homework. My other children were required to adhere to a 9 p.m. bedtime at the same age. Obviously, this rule wouldn't work in Jordyn's situation. Sleep was sacrificed.

At about age 10, Jordyn finished practice at 8 p.m., but had to get up and go to school earlier. Currently, a typical day for Jordyn allows for very little discretionary time.

Typical Day for Jordyn

6:45 a.m.	Wake up, eat breakfast, get ready for practice
7:30 a.m.	Leave for morning workout
10:30 a.m.	Leave the gym and go directly to school
2:40 p.m.	Come home from school and get ready for practice
3:00 p.m.	Leave for night practice
8:30 p.m.	Return home, eat dinner, do homework, and shower
10:30 p.m.	Sleep

Since I can't add hours to Jordyn's day, I have learned to accept the fact that she only gets about eight hours of sleep a night, compared to the 9 or 10 my other kids get. What does cause me stress is when she stays up late on the weekends.

Girlfriend sleepovers were rarely an option for Jordyn because her rest was so important. She couldn't risk getting tired and worn down before going into another jam-packed week. Most of the time, she was fine with making that sacrifice. She occasionally would opt to stay up and do regular kid things during her free time.

In the earlier years, I had more parental authority than I do now and could force her to go to sleep. Now, during the teenage years, nagging her to go to bed just makes her want to stay up even later. Despite wanting to control her entire environment to ensure she could be at the top of her game, I had to let go and let Jordyn control her sleep schedule.

SLEEP BEFORE COMPETITION

As a competitive runner, I was never able to sleep before a race. I remember lying in hotel rooms listening to teammates' sounds of peaceful slumber as I rolled around calculating how many hours were left until it was time to wake up. The night before my first marathon, I slept about three hours. But guess what? I never fell asleep during a race!

In fact, I don't believe my performance was ever actually affected by the length of my sleep the night before a competition. What mattered more was the quality and amount of sleep I received during the weeks building up to that day. Staying rested a majority of the time is more important than a good night's sleep before a competition.

Thankfully, this lesson helped me immensely when Jordyn occasionally had trouble sleeping before a meet. I did everything in my power to create a conducive sleeping environment for her, whether at home or in a hotel. During most traveling meets, I would settle Jordyn in the room and then sit out in the hall so that she could go to sleep early. As she got older, she wouldn't care if I went down to the hotel lobby when she went to bed. Recently, when not staying with the National Team, we reserved a separate room for her so she could sleep without being interrupted.

ILLNESS– WHEN TO SKIP PRACTICE

Knowing when to skip practice isn't always clear-cut. Obvious symptoms such as a high fever or vomiting make the decision easy. Most of the time symptoms are milder and can be masked with over-the-counter medicines, making the choice of whether or not to train much more difficult.

It's a Catch-22 of sorts. No one wants her athlete to miss out on valuable training time, especially in a sport such as gymnastics where repetition of skills is so important. On the other hand, pushing too hard through an illness can not only make things worse, but also spread the sickness to others.

Fortunately, in the early years of Jordyn's gymnastics career, I went through nursing school and gained some valuable medical knowledge that gave me greater perspective on when to push through an illness and when to rest.

In the Wieber family, we categorized illnesses into two categories to help decide when Jordyn would attend practice. These are our personal guidelines and are not endorsed by any medical professional. **Be sure to follow a physician's recommendations when making decisions.**

"REALLY SICK"- SKIP PRACTICE

-Fever of more than 99 degrees

-Vomiting

-Overwhelming fatigue and could sleep all day

-Productive cough (coughing up mucus)

"COMING DOWN WITH SOMETHING"- TRY PRACTICE

-Nasal congestion or cold symptoms with no cough

-Exposed to illness and starting to feel tired

-Upset stomach but not vomiting

-Recovering from being "really sick" and has been taking an antibiotic for 24 hours or has not vomited for 24 hours

I can count on two hands the number of times Jordyn has missed practice due to illness. Sometimes skipping one day prevented her illness from getting worse and then causing her to miss several more days.

Generally speaking, high-level athletes such as gymnasts are healthy most of the time. Typical bouts of a cold or flu are bound to happen, as with all kids. Getting a jump on symptom control and extra rest at the first sign of sickness is key.

NUTRITION

With modern technology at our fingertips, nutrition information is only a click away. Typing in the word "nutrition" on a search engine elicits more than 448 million hits. Add to that hundreds of thousands of books and journal articles, magazines, classes and television shows and there is almost too much information to process.

Filtering the good information from the bad, the truth from the myths and good advice from the bad is not always easy. With the help of my registered dietitian friend and cohort, Louise Whitney, this chapter will provide some guidance and answers to specific questions related to nutrition for gymnasts.

SPECIAL TOPICS IN NUTRITION

Feeding the Wieber family has always been an interesting topic. My husband was born and raised on a dairy farm with the traditional meat-and-potato meal prepared and served to the family every night. I was raised by a Mediterranean-cooking, Lebanese mother. In 1982, for no real reason, I decided to become a vegetarian. For the next 10 years, I did not eat meat. A health scare in 1993 resulted in adding poultry to my diet. I have not had any red meat since 1982.

Add that to a family of four growing children and the fact that I hate to cook. Feeding the kids in their early years was easy. I would prepare a typical meat dish for the kids and my husband, then eat some kind of vegetarian meal myself.

As the kids got older, things became more complicated. By the age of 6, Jordyn practiced most nights of the week until 9:30 p.m. Our oldest daughter was in high school at that time and had her own crazy schedule with sports and other extra-curricular activities. Family meals became non-existent. I usually made a pan of something and left it on the stove.

Grocery shopping became complicated. At various points my son wanted to gain weight, Jordyn was trying to eat all organic and my youngest daughter just wanted chocolate cereal. I gave up trying to be a thrifty shopper and bought the kids what they wanted. That was probably my attempt to compensate for not being a great "cooking" mom.

Needless to say, my kids all became very self-sufficient at feeding themselves. Despite the differences in wants, likes and dislikes, there were a few nutritional areas that I closely monitored and enforced.

IRON AND CALCIUM

An experience with my oldest daughter, Lindsay, taught me a great lesson about nutritional deficits and the impact that can have on performance. Lindsay ran on the high school cross-country team. For the first two years of her cross-country season, she gradually improved her time for the 3.1-mile course. In her junior year, however, she started the season with her usual pace but gradually became slower and slower. By the middle of the season, she was almost four minutes slower. In one race, she wasn't able to finish. Cross-country running can be a mental challenge as much as it is physical. Lindsay assured me her training was going well, so I assumed this was a mental situation. We talked about mental blocks, anxiety, visualization and imagery. Nothing worked. Each race was worse and worse.

Finally, in desperation, I took Lindsay to the doctor for a check-up and some blood work. A couple of days later I received a phone call from the doctor saying Lindsay was suffering from severe anemia.

Anemia is a condition caused from low hemoglobin in the blood. Hemoglobin is responsible for carrying oxygen through the blood where it is delivered to working muscles and organs. A low amount of hemoglobin means a lower capacity for providing fuel, or oxygen, to her muscles during a run. Lindsay was immediately placed on an iron supplement and, by the end of the season, was running her usual pace.

The diagnosis of anemia was actually a good thing. There was a reason for her poor performance that was easily remedied. I found through my own research that young women are twice as likely to suffer from anemia due to menstrual bleeding. That, along with the fact that Lindsay had a vegetarian mother who didn't prepare red meat (a great source of iron) made complete sense. Since then, I have made a conscious effort to provide my family with red meat and other sources of iron.

Registered dietitian Louise Whitney pointed out that you don't want to supplement with iron pills unless there is a known deficiency. Too much iron, when it's not needed, can cause other problems.

Another story that has stuck with me through the years was that of Katie Teft, a former elite gymnast and U.S. National Team member. Katie shared with me that after making the U.S. National Team in 1993, she had some testing that indicated that she had a calcium deficiency. This was determined to be the ultimate cause of the 10 fractures in her feet and ankles during the course of her gymnastics career. After an eighth place finish at the U.S. Olympic Trials in 1996, Katie ultimately injured her back and was forced to leave the world of elite gymnastics.

With that story in the back of my mind, I was very conscious of Jordyn's calcium intake. Because Jordyn was not a big milk drinker, I gave her a chewable calcium tablet each day to ensure her needs were met. Once Jordyn was through puberty, I relaxed a bit on the calcium issue but was reminded by Louise that calcium consumption is always important. In fact, as the consumption of soda pop goes up in teens, the intake of milk typically goes down.

According to Whitney, soda pop, even if it's diet soda pop, should be absolutely taboo for gymnasts because it leaches the calcium from their bones. Calcium and phosphorus should be equal in the body for good bone health. When kids drink a lot of soda pop the phosphorus intake goes up at the same time that they are probably consuming less calcium. Not to mention, the jury is still out on the safety of artificial sweeteners.

the bottom line

Proper nutrition, healthy eating, and weight control don't have to be a nemesis for the parent of a gymnast. By following general nutritional guidelines recommended by the American Dietetic Association as illustrated on My Plate, you can be assured your daughter is eating right. Here are a few tips for getting through some of the bumps along the road related to health and nutrition.

- Be a good example for your daughter. The entire family, including you, should be eating well-balanced, nutritious meals. Don't make exceptions to the rules for other members of the family.

- Don't focus on scale weight. The scale doesn't tell you how much of body weight is coming from fat and how much is from lean tissue, organs, and bones. A muscular gymnast might weigh more than you'd expect. Focus on a healthy lifestyle and the healthy weight will follow.

- Moderation is the key. We are all human. Humans like sugar, fat and treats now and then. It's okay to splurge on an occasional treat as long as it's done in moderation. Creating "good foods" and "bad foods" puts foods into only two categories. Nutrition is not black and white. Rather, follow the My Plate guidelines and keep foods with low nutritional density to a minimum.

- Don't encourage dieting. Dieting is temporary. At some point the diet will come to an end, and any lost weight will be regained quickly unless nutritional habits have been improved. Rather than promoting quick weight loss, help your daughter focus on healthy nutrition and moderation so it becomes normal in her life.

An Interview with Registered Dietitian Louise Whitney

Louise Whitney is Registered Dietitian at Sparrow Health System in Lansing, Mich.

SPECIAL DIETARY NEEDS FOR GYMNASTS

RITA: **It is not difficult to find general nutrition recommendations for our children. But competitive gymnasts train between 15 and 30 hours a week. What special dietary needs might they have?**

LOUISE, RD: First of all, they need to make sure they don't get "carb phobic." A lot of myth information indicates carbohydrates as being bad, and the kids will get too heavy. Carbohydrates remain the body's preferred energy source, and the key is to focus on whole grains in cereals or breads or other grains like rice or pasta. Also make sure the gymnast is getting adequate sources of fruits and vegetables that provide another source of complex carbohydrates. Carbohydrates are the main energy source.

Protein intake is also important because the gymnast is still growing. Protein is needed as a baseline. Do gymnasts need extra protein to build strength? Most Americans get plenty of protein. When you are dealing with a special circumstance, like a vegetarian home, that may be another issue.

For an average person, 8/10 of a gram of protein per kilogram of body weight should be good. To determine your weight in kilograms, divide the body weight in pounds by 2.2. For athletes doing excessive strength training, I might bump this requirement up to 1 gram of protein per kilogram of body weight.

For example, a gymnast weighing 50 kg (a little over 100 pounds) should consume 50 grams of protein each day. Lean meats and lean cuts of beef or pork are the best sources of protein. Fish, baked, broiled or grilled, should be on the menu for everyone two times per week because they provide Omega-3 fatty acids that reduces the risk of heart disease.

A great resource for calculating nutrition needs is **www.choosemyplate.gov**. This site has a link to "The 10 Tips Nutrition Education Series" that you can't beat for nutritional information.

In terms of fat, not all fat is bad. All types of dietary fat- saturated or unsaturated- are easily stored as fat in the body if not burned off. But unsaturated fats are considered healthier and come from plant sources such as olive oil or canola oil. Saturated fats come from animal sources and can clog the arteries with plaque that ultimately can lead to heart disease.

JUNK FOOD

RITA How do you deal with kids wanting junk food? It's a constant battle in our house.

LOUISE, RD If you are focused on three to four servings of dairy, half your plate is fruits and vegetables, if you are getting good healthy choices for meat and protein, and you eat whole grains, then you shouldn't be hungry. If you respect your body and stop eating when you are full, you may not have room for the junk. Maybe one day a week the kids get to choose something that's not the greatest food.

RITA One day a week? I did that once a day!

LOUISE, RD Well, every mom knows her kid. The one thing you don't want to do when trying to help them eat healthy is to create a lot of battles. Nobody is going to win.

NUTRITIONAL SUPPLEMENTS

RITA We all want our athletic children to have an edge. I once considered having Jordyn try a nutritional supplement program that was promoted at a gymnastics meet. Are these supplements safe or necessary?

LOUISE, RD They are not necessary, and sometimes, they may not be safe. Here's the problem: you do need protein, but why do you need four times that much? Some nutrients can

continued...

Louise's Picks for Healthy Snacks

(T=tablespoon)

2 oz. whole-wheat pita with 2T hummus

3 oz. tuna (packed in water) mixed with 1T light mayo and 1 cup halved grape tomatoes

1 portion Greek yogurt with 2 graham crackers

1 medium apple sliced and spread with 1T peanut or almond butter

½ cup low fat cottage cheese and ½ cup fresh berries

½ toasted whole grain bagel with 1 triangle Laughing Cow cheese spread

1 cup mixed raw vegetables (green or red pepper strips, baby carrots, broccoli florets) with ¼ cup low fat vegetable dip

Slimwich sandwich bread with 2 ounces turkey and/or 1 ounce of cheese with tomato slices

Smoothie made with 6 ounces fat free yogurt, ½ cup berries, splash of juice and a sprinkle of nutmeg or cinnamon

Hardboiled egg with small whole-wheat muffin

be stored in the body and become toxic. If you are eating right, you don't need the extras. Spend the money on something else that's more worthwhile. The supplement is not going to provide the competitive edge. If you feel your gymnast needs a "booster," then give her a children's multi-vitamin. This will give you a boost with the nutrients just in case she missed something that day. You can always ask your doctor to screen for calcium, zinc or any other nutrient if you want to fixate on that but I hardly ever find deficiencies.

ENERGY BARS

RITA I would often buy energy bars for Jordyn when she needed a snack. What are your thoughts on energy bars?

LOUISE, RD Energy bars have a lot of calories, a lot of sugar and a lot of extra protein that kids don't need. What would be better than an energy bar would be a turkey sandwich on whole grain bread with mozzarella cheese, a glass of milk and an orange. People think energy bars are magic, but they still have calories.

WEIGHT GAIN

RITA Weight gain is a big concern for gymnasts as they reach puberty. How can a gymnast adjust her diet to avoid gaining excess weight?

LOUISE, RD Stay away from the fluff. Stay away from energy dense foods that are empty calories. Those are things like chips, cakes, candies, cookies, donuts, pasties, and junk food— processed food. Clean up your diet! If you eat close to nature, that is the goal. Sure, one day a week, or twice a week, you have a treat.

FAT-FREE FOODS

RITA What about the fat-free foods?

LOUISE, RD Fat-free doesn't mean calorie-free. It probably has a lot more sugar. What gymnasts need to do is use reduced fat. With milk, definitely use fat free or skim. The same goes with yogurt. If they want a snack, it would be better to pair a whole grain, fruit or vegetable with something with protein.

EATING DISORDERS

RITA: **I've heard more than one horror story about gymnasts and other young women who developed eating disorders, even anorexia nervosa. What are the signs of a developing eating disorder?**

LOUISE, RD: Signs of an eating disorder include a hyper fixation on food, refusing to eat or binging on food. Preventing an eating disorder involves helping your child pay attention to her body's signals of saying "I'm hungry." Sometimes people don't do that- they don't eat. Rather than skipping meals they should even eat more frequently but less food each time. If athletes' listen to messages from coaches or parents to lose weight, they think not eating is a way to lose weight. Then, weight becomes a battle. Sometimes it's control. If you have a child, for example, whose life is very controlled by the schedule, the things she can control include going to the bathroom, eating and sleeping. In these cases, the gymnast is striving for control over something in her life.

If a gymnast can learn about food, maybe with the help of a dietitian, they can learn how to make good choices and avoid negative consequences.

NUTRITION WEBSITES

RITA: **There is so much nutritional information available on the web. What are some of the best websites and resources for parents of gymnasts?**

LOUISE, RD: There are so many good sites out there. **Choosemyplate.gov**, as I mentioned, is my top choice. There are also great smart phone applications to help kids track their food intake so they can see the nutrition they are receiving.

CHAPTER SEVEN
preventing and treating injuries

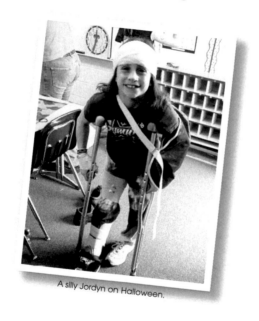

A silly Jordyn on Halloween.

A big scare came one morning about seven years ago when I was walking through Target. I dropped Jordyn off at morning practice an hour earlier. Seeing her coach's name on my caller ID sent a chill through my spine.

"I think I'm going to call it," John said when I answered. "I'm going to call an ambulance."

He was a little too calm for a full-blown emergency. I could tell by his contemplation that he wasn't sure an ambulance was necessary. Jordyn had landed on her head doing a vault drill and had some point tenderness in her upper cervical spine- an injury that could go from potentially serious to critical in minutes.

He said Jordyn was conscious, not in a lot of pain and could move all of her limbs, but he was worried about the tenderness she had when he palpated her neck. Not wanting to upset Jordyn with an ambulance, I told him to wait until I got there.

With a background as a personal trainer and exercise physiologist, I felt confident that Jordyn didn't need an ambulance. The gym keeps a supply of emergency equipment on hand so I placed a cervical collar on her neck and drove her to the emergency department myself. Looking back, this was probably not the best move!

Thankfully, her condition never worsened. We waited eight hours for the x-ray and CT scan. I knew she didn't have a spinal cord injury, but I was worried that she cracked her spine. A setback like that could greatly impact her entire gymnastics career. The diagnosis was a sprain. After another 48 hours in the c-collar and a week of rest, Jordyn was back to full practice.

A sport that requires many hours of rigorous training and complex physical movements increases the risk of injury. If your daughter is a gymnast, she may suffer an injury at some point. Many are minor, quick-healing sprains. Others can require months of healing and rehab. There are, however, many things that can be done to reduce the risk of injury.

Luckily, the office of Dr. Larry Nassar, the team physician for the U.S. women's team is only minutes from our home. Dr. Nassar has provided Olympic medical care for gymnasts for more 20 years first as an athletic trainer, then as a sports medicine physician. He is considered THE medical expert for the sport of women's artistic gymnastics.

AN INTERVIEW WITH DR. LARRY NASSAR

Larry Nassar, D.O. is the team physician for the U.S. Women's Gymnastics Team. He specializes in primary care sports medicine at the Michigan State University Sports Medicine Clinic.

COMMON GYMNASTICS INJURIES

RITA: What are the most common injuries for competitive gymnasts?

DR. LARRY: The most common injuries for competitive gymnasts are the foot/ankle and the wrist. This has remained a constant for several decades, and it is the same for men and women. After this comes the shoulder for men, and for women, it is variable, but frequently it is the back.

REDUCING THE RISK OF INJURIES

RITA: What can parents and/or gymnasts do to reduce the risk of an injury?

DR. LARRY: The coach plays a critical role in reducing the risk of injury. This is a lecture I give at many USA Gymnastics events. The coach can reduce the risk of injury by having a good understanding of how to progress a gymnast through each level, through each season, through each Olympic cycle, and through each preparation for a competition. A proper training plan is vital.

continued...

The coach also has to make sure the gym is safe, with proper equipment that is in good condition, with proper matting and use of training aids like pits and trampolines and other devices. The coach also needs to be aware of a gymnast's physical and mental fatigue. Injury increases when a gymnast is mentally and/or physically fatigued. The coach has to encourage proper nutrition and allow gymnasts to hydrate well in practice.

The gymnast first needs to be honest and recognize when she has a body part that is not responding properly. She must inform her coach and parent. Too often, a small injury turns into a large injury when a gymnast tries to ignore the injury and push through. A very common theme that occurs over and over again is that the gymnast is "afraid" to tell the coach. I try to educate the coaches to be more open with communication, and I tell the gymnasts that they need to tell the coach early on if they feel they have an injured body part.

SORENESS VS: INJURY

RITA How does a gymnast know if she has an injury and is not just "sore?" When and how do they tell the coach?

DR. LARRY I explain to the gymnasts that a significant injury is when they are trying to accomplish a skill, drill or conditioning exercise and their body part is not responding like it should. They need to tell the coach early on and not wait too long. They can use a series of phrases like, "coach, my ankle is hurting some, but I know I can do more" then "coach my ankle is hurting but I can try to do more" and finally, "coach, my ankle is hurting and I do not think I can do more." My hope is that with the first statement to the coach, the coach will pay greater attention and see if the gymnast is compensating or just not able to do the drill/skill properly due to the discomfort.

Once the coach sees the favoring or difficulty, then he or she needs to have the gymnast stop and move on to another drill/skill instead of having her do the drill/skill over and over again. Coaches need to realize that the gymnast possibly cannot do the drill/skill because of the injury and not because "she just does not like doing that skill/drill." The coach should respond by having the gymnast change the skill or stop the event. The gymnast needs to be able to request taping or bracing of an injury to protect her from further damage. She needs to be able to communicate with the coach and parent.

THE PARENT'S ROLE IN INJURIES

RITA I know sometimes gymnasts are hesitant to tell their parents when they have an injury. What is the parent's role in the case of an injured gymnast?

DR. LARRY The parents need to listen to their child and not be judgmental. The parent should not "coach" his or her own child, but be supportive. The parent needs to seek out proper medical care for their child in a timely fashion.

DEALING WITH CHRONIC INJURIES

RITA How could competitive gymnastics lead to chronic back or other chronic problems?

DR. LARRY Chronic injuries can occur from many situations: when the gymnast trains on poor equipment that does not absorb the forces well; has a training plan that is not appropriate for her body; does too much without adequate rest to recover properly before training again; not communicating with the coach when she has the start of an injury; and attempting to train through the early warning signs of pain and fatigue. Chronic injuries also occur when an athlete does not condition or rehabilitate well and allow an area to remain weak or too tight.

WHEN TO STOP GYNASTICS DUE TO INJURY

RITA What types of conditions or serious injury would cause you to recommend that an athlete does not engage in the sport of gymnastics?

DR. LARRY A gymnast with an injury that may prevent her from having the required motion and strength should stop the sport. In addition, if the gymnast sustains an injury that places her at risk for continued pain and progression or degeneration of a body part that will create significant pathology as she ages, she should retire from the sport.

TRAINING THROUGH INJURIES

RITA Sometimes competitive gymnasts train with back braces, foot boots or even wearing a cast - why is that?

DR. LARRY In many sports athletes continue to train with braces/splints/casts

continued...

on as long as the device does not prevent them from safely performing the skills and drills. The ultimate goal would be to allow an injury to heal and still keep the athlete in good condition. Returning to the sport in decreased condition may actually increase the chance of further injury. A gymnast should not train with a cast or brace when it prevents him or her from safely and effectively performing the drill skill or if it reduces the ability for the injury to heal properly.

GYMNASTICS AND GROWTH

RITA: Does competitive gymnastics stunt growth?

DR. LARRY: Gymnasts are short since that is what is needed to be successful in the sport. Therefore, shorter people select to do the sport. Once they begin to grow taller, they usually choose to do another activity. Taller children leave the sport and the shorter ones continue. It is like saying that playing basketball makes you taller.

PEDIATRICIAN VS. SPORTS MEDICINE DOCTOR

RITA: Can a family physician or pediatrician deal properly with gymnastics injuries or should a sports physician always be seen?

DR. LARRY: The best physician for a gymnast to see is a physician that has current knowledge of the appropriate diagnostic skills and appropriate use of lab and imaging studies. Physicians need to be current with the appropriate manner to treat the injury. Many of the best surgeons who treat athletes have no specific training in sports but are excellent diagnosticians with excellent skills and have advanced treatment protocols that allow the athlete to respond well to their care. The bottom line is that the gymnast should see a highly skilled physician with a good reputation for their care of patients.

real-life lessons

Jordyn's neck scare was not the first injury she suffered in the past 10 years, and I'm sure it won't be the last. As a mom, dealing with the injuries was not often my best display of patience and faith. Yet, with each injury, I gained knowledge and experience that helped me cope with the frustration and disappointment.

The most serious injury Jordyn suffered was a badly torn hamstring. Thankfully, an MRI revealed the hamstring muscle had not pulled completely away from the bone where it attaches, which would have made the injury even more severe. It had, however, pulled enough to cause swelling and irritation at the insertion site. Healing takes time in hamstring injuries. Rushing back too quickly could result in a re-injury. Weekly checks with Dr. Nassar and two or three sessions of physical therapy helped, but Jordyn was still unable to compete for 14 months. During her recovery period, Dr. Nassar and John Geddert planned a detailed progression of gradually adding skills back in to her training.

Aside from the hamstring, Jordyn recovered quickly from most of her other injuries. In retrospect, a few of the injury stories can actually be spun to contain a touch of humor.

"STRADDLING" THE BEAM

About eight years ago on carpool pick-up duty, I got to the gym early to watch the last hour of practice. After finding a spot in the viewing area, I did the "Where's Jordyn" and searched for my daughter among the little colorful leotard-laden gymnasts. That night, Jordyn was easy to spot - she was wearing shorts over her leo.

"Why is Jordyn wearing shorts?" I asked the group of fervently-watching moms.

"She took a spill on beam doing her series and then went in to the bathroom for a while and came out with shorts on after that," one of the moms replied.

I sat and watched Jordyn finish without incident. She must have ripped her leotard, I thought. A ripped leotard would have been welcomed after I found out what really happened. Jordyn told me she straddled the beam, or, in layman's terms, landed from a tumbling move with the beam in her crotch. She said she cut herself and that's why she was wearing shorts.

I escorted Jordyn to the restroom to take a look at the damage to find a five-centimeter deep laceration that clearly required sutures. Jordyn received her seven stitches in the crease of her crotch. Needless to say, split jumps took a back seat at practice as she healed up for the next 10 days.

Gym mom lesson learned: *Your daughter may love a sport so much that she covers a deep sub-cutaneous laceration with a pair of shorts and keeps training.*

THE FAT LIP AND BIG NOSE

The day before Jordyn's eighth-grade farewell dance, the premier social event of the year, she had an untimely snafu at practice. Upon my arrival at the gym, many moms asked me if I'd seen Jordyn yet. The buzz was that Jordyn hit her face on the bar doing a release move. As long as she was walking and talking, I wasn't too concerned.

Jordyn at her 8th grade farewell dance, post face plant into the bars.

Inappropriately, I actually laughed when Jordyn finally emerged from the locker room. Not only was her nose double in size, her upper lip was so swollen she couldn't move it. It almost looked fake. Jordyn was a trouper at her dance the next night, posing for hundreds of pictures despite her awkward appearance.

Gym mom lesson learned: *Several layers of cover-stick can hide most stages of bruising.*

THE FIRST SPRAINED ANKLE INCIDENT

In 2006, Jordyn's short-lived Level 10 career consisted of four meets. Lucky for us, the state championships was held in East Lansing, just minutes from our home. It was a rare chance for many of our friends and relatives to see Jordyn compete after hearing so much about her rapid progress in the sport.

About 30 friends and relatives, including Jordyn's teacher, filled the stands ready to be wowed by her talent. What none of them noticed was that Jordyn landed short on a tumbling pass during warm-ups. She made it through bars and beam with a fall. Unfortunately, her ankle was really bothering her during floor touch warm-ups, and she had to withdraw from the meet. For some reason, I felt responsible for the fact that so many supporters came to the meet, paid a $10 entry fee, and Jordyn wasn't able to complete. It wasn't obvious what had happened so I tried to explain the situation to all 30 friends and family, who really didn't understand the sport of gymnastics. They were all gracious, complimenting Jordyn on what they were able to watch and wished her a quick recovery.

Gym mom lesson learned: *Your friends and family come to support your gymnast whether they finish the meet or not. Don't feel responsible for their entertainment.*

THE ELBOW BURSITIS

What was probably Jordyn's very first injury occurred when she was 7 years old. At this time, Jordyn's main focus was TOPs training that involved an inordinate amount of strength training and conditioning. At the same time, Jordyn was participating in the Presidential Physical Fitness testing at her elementary school. One of the measures of strength was a push-up. Needless to say, unlike most of the other elementary school children, Jordyn was trained for this. The second-grade boys' school record was 130 pushups. Jordyn, who must not have realized she was a girl, decided she needed to break that record and performed 135 pushups. About a week later, Jordyn's elbow was bothering her at the gym. A visit to Dr. Nassar yielded a diagnosis of bursitis in the elbow joint from repetitive motion. To this day, I would guess Jordyn thinks that injury was worth it.

Gym mom lesson learned: *Competitive gymnasts are competitive kids, especially in gym class.*

rips and cracked toes

A few years into her gymnastics career, we realized that Jordyn would never be a hand or foot model. Her delicate, soft palms took a beating once she started working on the uneven bars. For anyone who has ever had a skin rip from shoveling or raking, you can understand the painful, stingy, burning feeling a small tear can cause. There were nights when Jordyn would have trouble falling asleep due to the pain of a rip. With the help of Dr. Nassar and advice from seasoned gymnasts to put bag balm on her palms at night, Jordyn made it through the rip-era. Today, thick calluses on her palm help to prevent frequent rips (see inset).

The Treatment of "RIPS" on the Hands

By Larry Nassar, DO, ATC

P revention of infection is the first thing to consider when treating a rip. I have seen improperly treated rips develop cellulitis (a bad skin infection) and required intravenous (IV) antibiotics for treatment of the wound. The most important thing to do after a rip occurs is to wash the hand with warm water and a mild soap. The latest medical research shows that soap and warm water is more effective in treating wounds than using Betadine (providone iodine) or hydrogen peroxide. Hydrogen peroxide should not be used as a general wound cleaner unless recommended by a physician. It has been determined that hydrogen peroxide is too caustic for the wound and destroys healthy cells and can actually delay healing. Betadine has also been shown to be too strong and can damage cells when applied to a wound. However, diluting the Betadine or hydrogen peroxide with water first to a 50/50 solution is OK to use. However, the most effective way of cleaning wounds is by irrigating it well with water and washing it with warm soapy water.

Once the rip has been washed and dried to prevent infection, then a sterile bandage should be applied. The type of sterile bandage depends on the severity of the rip and the cost of treating the wound. The inexpensive way of treating minor rips is by applying an antibiotic ointment (Neosporin or Bacitracin) to a sterile bandage and covering the wound with this bandage. Change the bandage when it becomes wet.

No matter what type of dressing used to cover a wound, signs of infection need to be assessed. These signs of infection include: a foul odor,

continued...

pus or yellowish discharge (exudate), redness (erythema), and fever. If these signs develop the wound should be evaluated by a physician for further cleaning and the use of antibiotics.

The gymnast may try any of the above methods to help them train through the rips but rip prevention is important too. Maintain your grips in good condition. Keep the calluses on your hands trimmed. Avoid swimming or keeping your hands in water for a long period of time since I have seen many rips related to this. Pay attention to your hands to keep them working well.

Treatment of Rips

The treatment of rips has become a part of gymnastics folklore through the years. There are many treatments that have been tried and sworn to be effective through the years. For example:

• Preparation H or other hemorrhoid ointments have been used to reduce tissue swelling and some have a topical anesthetic to help numb the rip.

• Bag Balm, which is a veterinary balm, applied to cows' utters because they have a tendency to crack/split. Bag Balm is used to help treat fresh rips or as a hand conditioner to prevent rips.

• A small balloon taped over the rip may help. The friction generated between the bars and the tape causes the balloon to rub against its inner surfaces and prevents friction between the balloon and the rip.

• Tuff Skin (a taping base) sprayed onto a fresh rip has been reported to help heal rips - this is not recommended.

• Another fairly common treatment is soaking the freshly ripped hand in a 10 percent bleach in water solution-this also is not recommended.

- The old standby is covering the hands with a hand lotion, vitamin E or aloe vera at night while sleeping and protecting the bed sheets by wearing gloves or socks over the hands. Please, use a non-perfumed hand lotion since the perfume is alcohol based.

- Gibson Gymnastics sells DAT Sticks which is a series of three balms: a callous stick used prior to workouts to promote toughening of calluses, a condition stick which is used at night to keep calluses smooth and pliable; and a rip stick used to help heal fresh rips. (Www.gibsonathletic.com)

- Dunlap makes a skin protector called "Compeed" which can be used in practice to protect the fresh rip and also helps to heal these rips. This can be found in many sporting goods stores and bicycle shops.

- Neoprene rubber wrist bands are used to prevent rips on the wrists from dowel grips.

- Of course the tape grip made out of white trainer's tape to protect a rip is a standard, but I recommend using Johnson & Johnson Elastikon elastic tape instead

- Trimming calluses (with a corn and callus shaver) is important to help prevent rips from occurring.

- DuoDERM and Nova Derm sterile occlusive dressings and Op-sight and Bioclusive transparent moisture vapor permeable hypoallergenic viral barriers.

Cracked Toes
By Larry Nassar, DO, ATC

Toe splits are a very painful problem for the artistic gymnast. The force that a gymnast's foot sustains is exceptionally high. So high in fact that the force of impact of the gymnast's toes can create a sudden tear in the skin at the attachment of the toes to the foot. Most commonly, this happens at the big toe. However, this can occur at any toe and sometimes at more than one toe at a time. It is important to properly care for these splits to allow them to heal as quickly as possible because they are a very painful and annoying condition for the gymnast.

Treatment of split toes begins with cleaning the split to prevent infection. Wash the area with warm soap and water. Make sure you clean all the chalk and dirt out of the split. A topical antibiotic cream can then be applied. Bacitracin® is a good choice to use. A bandage may be applied to keep the area clean out of the gym.

In the gym, the use of a bandage is not very practical because it commonly rolls into the wound or slips off. I have tried suturing the split, gluing the split, suturing and then applying glue over the split; however, all of these methods have failed to keep the split closed. As soon as the gymnast attempts to tumble (especially on the balance beam) the forces on the toe just rip the wound open again. Waiting until the wound fully heals before tumbling again is an option. However, this may not be practical if the gymnast splits the toe in a competition or just before a competition.

For more information on taping toes for practice and competition see a reprint of the article from "USA Gymnastics"; Taping Split Toes; Larry Nassar; July – August 2010 at www.usagym.org.

Jordyn's feet and toenails are another story. Cracks in the creases of her toes and broken toenails from random mishaps in the gym make for a rather hideous sight. Occasional pedicures are a welcome treat. Unfortunately, prior to Jordyn's appearance on the "Today" show in 2011, there was not time for a pedicure. Her feet were the last of her concerns having to perform some beam moves in front of live cameras out on the plaza at Rockefeller Center in New York City. During the post beam interview, the host, Savannah Guthrie, joked about the state of Jordyn's feet as the camera panned in for a close up. Thankfully, Jo managed a sense of humor about this and didn't bother with a pedicure prior to her next television appearance. There are plenty of years left in her life for attractive feet.

the bottom line

Injuries are part of every sport. Our family has dealt with as many injuries with our football-playing son as we have with our gymnast daughter. So, when fear of injury or frustration overtakes my mind and the quality of my sleep, I remind myself of these lessons I have learned over the years.

> **Lesson #1: Trust the coaches.** Good coaches are experts at knowing how to teach and advance a skill. Good coaches know how to spot a gymnast on difficult skills. Good coaches have set up a safe gym with the proper, protective padding and equipment. Let them do their job.

> **Lesson #2: Accidents happen.** Even with the best coaches in the world, accidents happen. That's part of life and part of every

sport. No amount of worry and stress will prevent a random accident. If it happens, deal with it.

Lesson #3: Be patient with recovery. When an acute or chronic injury occurs, rehabilitation and recovery take time. Rushing the gymnast back into competition could result in a re-injury and even longer break. Waiting 14 months for Jordyn's hamstring to completely heal was a true test of patience. Hamstring injuries have a high incidence of re-injury, so knowing her long-term goals, rushing the recovery wasn't an option. In time, injuries heal.

Lesson #4: Be sure your gymnast follows the directions in her recovery. When the doctor or therapist prescribes home activities, such as icing, stretching or exercises, be sure they get done. Completing these activities at home isn't fun and, therefore, can easily be "forgotten" by the gymnast. This is a great time for the parent to step in.

Lesson #5: Control the things you can control, and then relax. Your role as a mom is to keep your gymnast healthy and happy so she can be in top form. A tired, hungry, unhappy child will have trouble focusing at practice and that is when accidents happen. Do your part to keep her life in balance, then relax and let her do her thing.

CHAPTER EIGHT
mind games

Jordyn in a moment of contemplation at her first international assignment, the Jr. Pan American Games in Guatamala.

W hen Jordyn was 7 years old and just beginning her competitive years, I thought I held the key to her mind. She was still young enough to listen to me so I took full advantage of her impressionable psyche. The night before her meets I would lay in bed with her and talk through her entire competition so she could visualize herself hitting all of her routines. I would tell her to only allow positive thoughts of success and that her body would follow her mind. Whether or not those quiet moments of imagery really made any difference in the course of her competitive years is unknown. I would like to think that some of the tips and talks I had with Jordyn made a positive difference.

Since those early years, I haven't broached the subject of what goes through Jordyn's mind before or during a competition. When younger gymnasts ask her, she tells them that she gets excited before a competition not really nervous. She says she is excited to finally show off her routines after all of her hard work.

What goes through the minds of athletes during an intense competition is an intimate subject. I'm not sure if it's difficult to put into words, or such an intensely private matter that Jordyn has difficulty answering questions about the topic. There's no doubt that the ability to compete in gymnastics, at any level, is admirable. Imagine one shot at performing combinations of difficult physical skills that took years to master, in front of judges, parents, friends and coaches. For top-level elite gymnasts, add television cameras tracking every move for the world to see.

Such experiences provide an indispensable lesson in handling pressure! Imagine your gymnast with future job interviews, public speaking, test taking, performing tasks under timed pressure. With such valuable practice handling competitive pressure, surely, these situations will be met with less anxiety and discomfort. There won't be many challenges in life that ruffle a former competitive gymnast.

Every now and then, the mind can play unexpected games on the body. A bad fall in practice, for example, can reduce confidence in a particular skill that can intensify nervousness at competition time. A growth spurt can alter the gymnast's center of gravity and cause an old, easy skill to suddenly become difficult and inconsistent. Even great success can increase expectations and pressure to a new, dysfunctional level.

The psychology of a sport such as gymnastics is extremely complex. Not only must a gymnast possess incredible physical athleticism, but also she must be able to complete the difficult skills on demand during a competition. It doesn't get much more psychologically challenging.

While providing incentives and rewards may help keep some gymnasts motivated and happy, sometimes true psychological issues develop that can't be fixed with a prize. I had the pleasure of talking with Dr. Alison Arnold about the mental side of gymnastics.

As a mental toughness coach to USA Gymnastics since 1997, "Doc Ali" has worked with thousands of gymnasts around the world. She has also worked for U. S. A Figure Skating, Australia's ski team and various Olympic and professional athletes, along with many of the top NCAA gymnastics teams. She's the creator of "The Athlete Warrior Mental Toughness Workbook" and "Head Games WebCamp," a live, online mental toughness-training program (www.headgames.ws).

Doc Ali provided some great tips for dealing with the emotional and psychological side of gymnastics.

AN INTERVIEW WITH
DR. ALISON ARNOLD

Dr. Alison Arnold has been the mental toughness coach to USA Gymnastics since 1997, and has worked with 10 NCAA teams. She has the first on-line mental toughness program for gymnasts and numerous mental toughness books and workbook. See **www.headgames.ws** for more information.

INCENTIVES AND PRIZES

RITA: What are your thoughts on parent's providing incentives or prizes for accomplishments?

DOC ALI: In America today, so many kids' self-esteems are based upon what they HAVE rather than who they ARE. I think it's important to redirect athletes back to how they feel about their accomplishments rather than some materialistic payoff. "Wow, you made that skill! You must be proud. Let's celebrate!" If we continue to "bribe" our children with "if you do this, I will buy you that," they don't develop the internal motivation to do their best simply because it feels good, and the prizes have to become bigger and bigger! If you're a parent, I would say, "Don't open that can of worms. Before you know it, you'll be in it for a car. "

PUNISHING POOR PERFORMANCE

RITA: What are your thoughts on parents punishing or verbally reprimanding for a poor performance?

DOC ALI: When dealing with a competitive athlete, a parent's job is to give his or her child love, belief and a shelter in the storm. High-level athletes already put extreme pressure on themselves and usually train with coaches, who also have high expectations. A parent must "neutralize" the pressure triangle (parent-coach-athlete) by supporting the athlete in both good and bad performance. Allow your child to vent his/her disappointment to you in a safe place where she is not afraid of anger or repercussions.

After she vents, you can always ask her the magic question, "What do you want to do differently next time?" This helps her get out of the victim role and back into the driver's seat.

Punishment from a parent after poor performance will only lead to more pressure, tension and fear of failure in the athlete. I can guarantee that!

MENTAL BLOCKS

RITA: **How can gymnasts work through issues of a "mental block" (i. e. : being scared to do a skill)?**

DOC ALI: There are many techniques I use to help gymnasts work through fears and blocks, some simple and some complex. Here are a few that are the tip of the iceberg.

The first thing I do is determine the source of the fear. Sometimes, it is easily explained like a fall or injury, and sometimes, it originates from a deeper source like fear of failure. Next, all fear comes from the mind, so I lock the mind down on cue words that keep it busy and mechanical. I also may help the athlete create a confidence ladder which is a progressions ladder putting them back in control of the skill. A mental block is usually a stuck thought pattern or neural pathway. One of the most important things I do is utilize new therapeutic techniques that can "re-program" how the athlete thinks about the skill.

DEALING WITH FRUSTRATION AND DISAPPOINTMENT

RITA: **What is the best way for parents to deal with their gymnast's frustration or disappointment if things aren't going well at practice or competition?**

DOC ALI: Put on your shrink hat and play psychologist! Listen to your child. Acknowledge her feelings. Validate her reality. In many psychology schools, this is called LAV-ing a client. After your athlete shares her feelings, always direct her to action. Don't let her stay in a passive role. Help her create a plan where she takes responsibility and control to move things in a new direction.

COMPETITION NERVES

RITA: **How do you help gymnasts work through fears of competition or nerves?**

DOC ALI: It's very important for gymnasts to see competition as an opportunity to shine. Each of us has an internal state of being where we perform our best. It is our own individual "zone. "It's the place where everything seems effortless, smooth and flows. I have each gymnast create her own ideal mental state for competition and then teach her tools using breathing, self-talk, and body language that help her get to that state. Gymnasts need to have emotional control and flexibility. Using breathing, brain, body language and belief, she can step into her competition bubble whenever she needs to! This takes practice, but it's definitely in her control!

DEALING WITH PRESSURE

RITA **As you may know, the world of competitive gymnastics is filled with very competitive people: gymnasts, parents and coaches. This competitiveness often leads to more pressure. How do you help athletes deal with the pressure they may put on themselves or from their parents or coaches?**

DOC ALI It's essential that an athlete feel like she is doing gymnastics for herself and sets her own personal goals. When you have a goal like "going all out at this competition," you can take the focus away from the outcome and what you could GET out of the competition. Put the emphasis on what the gymnast is going to do and what she is GIVING to the competition. Looking at competition as a show or a chance to demonstrate your gymnastics gift helps move from a pressure focus to one of gratitude and joy.

WINNING STRATEGIES

RITA **What strategies do you teach gymnasts for helping them reach their full potential (i. e. : visualization, goal setting)?**

DOC ALI I teach gymnasts a multitude of strategies helping them train their mind in order to perform their best. Mostly, I focus on clear intention, mental consistency and emotional control. Clear intention is creating a specific vision of the gymnast they want to be including goals, mannerisms and specific elements. Mental consistency is learning how to control thinking and not go on the crazy, negative, anxiety producing "field trips" of the monkey mind. Learning to control thoughts and not believe negative thinking is a skill with drills that must be practiced and mastered. There is nothing better than a gymnast coming to me and saying, "I beat my beast (negative) thoughts! I didn't go on the field trip! "

Mental consistency also includes locking down the mind on words and phrases to keep it on task as if it were a young child. Emotional control and recovery is getting to one's ideal mental state, and bringing her mind back to that state after adversity. There is so much adversity in this sport that can trigger the mind! From a fall, to a fear to coaches' moods, it's important a gymnast doesn't let those external pressures completely infect her mental state. I use drills, arm sets, visualization, video, written exercises, and other tools to train these mental toughness skills.

INBORN POTENTIAL

RITA: **How much do you believe the ability to handle the pressure of competition is inborn or part of the gymnasts natural personality or character?**

DOC ALI: Just as some gymnasts are naturally stronger or have more flexibility than others, it is also common that some gymnasts seem to have more natural mental toughness. This may come from early childhood parental messages or the style of coaching. Never the less, all gymnasts can learn to handle the pressure of competition with a little mental training. I have seen many athletes wilt under pressure, who become beasts in competition after learning some tools to get their minds and bodies where they need to be. I like to believe we can learn to be better and better in all things with a little effort, at least, I hope so!

BEST ADVICE FOR PARENTS

RITA: **What is the most important advice you would give to parents when dealing with a competitive gymnast?**

DOC ALI: Always remember, you are the foundation of your child's self-esteem. In our achievement-focused world, many kids define themselves by what they DO rather than who they ARE. When an athlete's identity is all about performance, it can create too much pressure and fear of failure.

Parents need to put energy into praising an athlete's character as well as performance, especially if their child is showing signs of fear of failure, a debilitating amount of self-criticism, or hesitancy in competition. Praising character means noticing things like hard work, optimism, leadership, compassion and other qualities that reflect the essence of who the child really is on the inside. Of course, you will still praise achievement, "I'm so proud of you for winning bars," but add a character component too, "but what I'm really proud of is how you were the first one to give your teammate a hug after her beam routine. "

inside the mind of the gym mom

While it's unimaginable to me to handle the psychological weight of being a competitive gymnast, I'm here to tell you it's no cakewalk being the mother of one. I've seen mothers cry, rock, shake, yell, leave the arena or not enter the arena. As much as it intrigues me to observe mothers watching her daughter compete, I don't want anyone watching me.

I'm not the picture of calm like my husband. He coolly sits in his assigned seat for the entire meet and rarely changes his facial expression. Anyone who knows me knows that I am a tad high strung. Sitting during the competition isn't always option for me. I need to pace, walk and preferably, hide. I'm an anxious mess.

In Australia at the 2011 Pacific Rim meet I tried to sit and watch like a normal spectator. My nervous energy manifested itself into wriggling and jiggling my legs as I sat. Mid-way through the meet the woman behind me gently tapped me on the shoulder and said, in her very Australian accent, "Excuse me, could you please stop wriggling. "I knew that wasn't an option for me, so I changed seats.

At the 2011 World Championships in Tokyo, I was probably the most nervous. During the team competition, each team is allowed three athletes to compete on each event. All three of the scores count toward the team score. Obviously, no one wants his or her child to be the one who falls and loses the whole competition for the entire team. The pressure the athletes must feel is unimaginable. The pressure I felt was paralyzing. At one point, I took to rocking back and forth while watching her compete on bars. I didn't realize I was standing right next to the British media who were providing the commentary for the live feed. Shortly after the meet, I noticed a number of text messages coming to my phone from my friends telling me the British commentators mentioned me: "Wieber's mother is rocking to-and-fro, wringing her hands." Meanwhile, Dave sat calmly in his assigned seat.

RITUALS AND SUPERSTITIONS

From the very beginning, I hold a handful of charms while Jordyn competes. Most are religious charms: crosses, angels and a finger rosary. The ritual has gone beyond just holding the charms. It now makes a difference when I have them in my pocket versus when I hold them and, in which hand I hold them. I also need to do at least one cycle of the rosary before each event. Most meet days I try to go for a run where I take the finger rosary and recite the Hail Marys and Our Fathers for the entire duration of my run. My superstitions as a gym mom do more to keep my mind occupied than anything else, especially since I have absolutely no control over Jordyn when she's competing.

Many athletes have pre-competition rituals and superstitions. They provide not only a calming effect but also an element of control and a sense of familiarity. Some rituals border on the bizarre: one pro hockey player would dip his stick in the toilet before each game; a pro baseball player would eat four pieces of black licorice per inning and then brush his teeth between each inning; a pro basketball player trimmed his fingernails with nail clippers on the bench during games.

It's very common to see athletes with less peculiar rituals, such as wearing the same socks, eating the same meal, bouncing the ball a designated number of times before play, or doing the sign-of-the-cross before competing. While we've never encouraged superstitions and rituals for Jordyn, some innocent actions developed into superstitions in my own mind.

When Jordyn began competing at Level 5, my husband and I would jokingly tell her to "Open Up a Can" before she competed. We explained to her that this was a common funny line used in several movies. A few weeks later, I happened upon a can of actual "Whoop Ass" energy drink sold at a convenience store. I bought it, drank it, and then gave it to Jordyn as a joke. She carried that empty can of "Whoop Ass" in her competition bag for years. I'm not sure if it was a superstition for her or if she just never cleaned out her bag. Either way, I felt a little calmer knowing it was there.

In 2007, when Jordyn was competing at Level 10, I started a silly superstition with Jordyn involving Skittles candy. Before each meet I would give Jordyn five Skittles, one for balance, one for no falls, one for sticking her landings, one for power and one for confidence. I had this ridiculous sense of power and control with this ritual. I'm pretty sure Jordyn was just in it for the candy.

When we were in Kansas City for Jordyn's first elite meet, the U. S. Classic, I realized after she went off with her coaches to warm-up that we had forgotten the Skittles ritual. In a panic, I tracked down her coach, gave him five Skittles to give to Jordyn and told him I'd explain later. Thankfully, Jordyn ended up qualifying to her first Visa Championships that day, but I'm guessing that it had more to do with her talent than the Skittles.

BLESSINGS AND HUMBLENESS

One of the greatest perks of being a parent is watching your gymnast thrive. Teaching your child the importance of hard work and then watching her reap the rewards of her efforts brings great feelings of joy.

Even if the outcome did not match the success hoped for, seeing your child make a valiant effort is rewarding. No matter the outcome, the life lessons of tenacity, goal setting and effort are invaluable.

From the start of Jordyn's gymnastics career, and with all of our children in their own endeavors, we have taken time to pray with them and thank God for their talents. Every night before a competition, and again just before the meet, Jordyn and I would privately pray together that she would make God proud with how she used her talents. God blesses us all with talents and gifts, but it is up to us to put them to good use. This was an important lesson we wanted Jordyn to reap from her experience.

With God as the foundation of our lives, being humble is instinctive. Of course pride and joy exist for all parents, especially when their children accomplish great things. While there is a difference between sharing good news and bragging – modesty is always a priority for our family.

I'm not sure if it's because of the gritty tenacity required of the sport, but I have never met a cocky or arrogant gymnast. I am continually amazed by the many appreciative, considerate and respectful athletes I have met throughout the years.

WHAT GYMNASTS AND GYM MOMS SAID ABOUT RITUALS AND SUPERSTITIONS

Q: Do you or your daughter have any pre-competition rituals or superstitions?

A: Yes, I have two guardian angel pendants, a pocket prayer pendant (given to me by Rita Wieber!) and a bracelet with a cross. I always hold at least one of these things in my right hand during competition. I always close my eyes and pray during her competition routines – then just watch them on video when she's finished. I know I am more nervous than she is. (A friend and I once dug for an hour in Arizona for lucky stones, but tossed them after both our girls fell on beam!)

Tracy Cutler, Level 10 Mom, Grand Rapids, Michigan

A: There were only two things that I can think of in this category, but they did not determine my performance. My ponytail had to be really tight, and the ponytail could not be long enough to touch my eyes when it went over my head or wrapped around the side during jumps. (It hurt if it whipped me in the eyes)

My dad would always wish me good luck by trying to push my hands down while I stood in a tight body squeeze with my hands over my head. We somehow felt that it made sure that my body was ready, kind of silly but fun.

Gigja, Former Gymnast

A: We always prayed for safety for all the competitors and that she would do her best. She would include a prayer for her teammates to not get in trouble by their parents for not winning.

Gym Mom, Haslett, Michigan

CHAPTER NINE
the next stage

Before you know it, the "leash" is gone.

I t's not only natural and common, it's adorable to hear new, and young gymnasts express their dreams of competing in the Olympics. Gymnastics is the most watched sport of the summer Olympics. It's chilling, thrilling and amazing to watch. It leaves an imprint in the minds of every gymnast. Becoming an Olympic gymnast is a reality for a very small number of girls. While competing at this level is possible, there are many other long-term options for gymnasts. Dreams of the Olympics should never be squashed. There will be girls who attain that goal. On the other hand, there are many other ambitions to which gymnasts can aspire.

For example, a college scholarship, a career in coaching or even seeking a profession or hobby that utilizes the specialty skills of a gymnast are all possibilities. I know former gymnasts who have gone on to enjoy careers in kinesiology, physical therapy, biomechanics, professional dance and performance, and choreography, all initially sparked by their experience in gymnastics.

elite gymnastics

I first heard the term "elite" gymnastics when Jordyn was 8 years old. She, along with a few other gymnasts, was selected by her coach to begin morning workouts a couple of days a week in addition to the regular 23 hours of evening gymnastics. The group was touted to become the next batch of elite gymnasts produced by Twistars Gymnastics Club. Not knowing much about elite gymnastics, we welcomed the opportunity for Jordyn to train in this special group. It was an honor to be selected. Jordyn was thrilled to be in the group. The school was cooperative and flexible with her new schedule. Dave and I were willing to juggle our jobs to get her to and from the extra practice.

A couple of years went by and the extra training paid off. Jordyn progressed to Level 10 by age 10 and placed second at the JO National Championships. Our choice, at this point, was to continue as a Level 10 gymnast for seven more years or progress to elite gymnastics. Everything happened so quickly I didn't have much time to explore what we were getting into. The differences between JO and elite gymnastics were much greater than I anticipated.

Becoming an elite gymnast meant going in a different direction than everyone else at the gym. No longer would Jordyn be on the same training path. No longer would she compete in the JO state, regional or national competitions. She would train harder and longer and compete less. Not knowing any other gymnasts in this position at our gym, I was a bit leery of the reaction this would bring from gymnasts and gym families.

The decision to allow Jordyn to pursue elite gymnastics wasn't simple. We were happy that she was talented enough to have the option, but the next step impacted the family and required serious consideration. In the gym, focus would be on learning more difficult skills and working on perfecting the execution. For example, a step back after a tumbling pass in JO gymnastics is allowed, while it is a deduction in elite gymnastics. A fall is a half-point deduction in JO and a full point in elite. The stakes are higher, and the scoring is tighter. The scoring, in fact, is totally different for elite gymnastics. Rather than a 10.0 maximum score, gymnasts earn an execution score of up to 10.0 added to the difficulty score of their routines, which is unlimited.

What concerned me most about elite gymnastics was that with the greater difficulty in skills came a higher risk for injury. Up to this point, Jordyn was used to competing in at least 10 meets per season. In the elite world, gymnasts must earn the privilege to compete internationally by verifying readiness to Martha Karolyi, the U.S. women's team

WOMEN'S ELITE/PRE-ELITE/TOPS PROGRAM OVERVIEW

The Elite Program is designed to provide competitive experiences for athletes aspiring to the national team or the pre-elite training squad. The national teams (senior and junior) are selected from the Visa Championships each year. These athletes represent the United States in International competitions.

The national team size can be up to 28 athletes. To address our country's needs and mirror the quad age requirements, the junior and senior team sizes will change each year. The support programs for the national team members will be included in the National Team Handbook and will be presented each year at the national team meeting after championships.

To ensure that support funds are awarded to those athletes who are representing our country at the highest-level meets:

• The senior funding slots will be determined after the final selection of the World or Olympic Team and the remaining slots are awarded by the rank order at Visa Championships.

• The junior funding slots will be determined from the rank order established at Visa Championships.

Regional and national elite clinics, training camps and competitions are conducted throughout the year to provide educational opportunities and the highest level of technique development to both athletes and coaches working within the elite program. Coaches who have an athlete that they believe is ready for the international elite level competition may submit a DVD or video link ...

...to the national team coordinator and request admission to a developmental, open, pre-elite, or national team training camp. If accepted, all costs associated with their attendance at camp are the responsibility of the gymnast and coach.

The Talent Opportunity Program (TOP) is under the direction of the national pre-elite committee, with assistance from the national coaching staff and the national team coordinator. This program provides early screening and identification of talented athletes. The TOP program offers state and national testing along with clinic opportunities and educational materials for its participants.

TOP program athletes are NOT classified as "elite" athletes.

Each year after the national championships, coaches' representatives are elected by their peers to the international elite committee (IEC), which works closely with the national team coordinator to develop a strong training program for elite athletes.

Each region has an elected representative to the national pre-elite committee (NPEC) who is responsible for the development and growth of the pre-elite program. The women's program director, in conjunction with the regional pre-elite chairman, appoints a TOP state manager for the development and growth of the Talent Opportunity Program within their state. For those clubs entering the elite/pre-elite program for the first time, it is advised that they contact their national pre-elite committee chairman for the most current and accurate information.

coordinator. Most elite gymnasts only compete a handful of times each year.

Financially, the impact of elite gymnastics would be greater. If Jordyn did not earn a spot on the U.S. National Team, we would be responsible for funding trips to the Ranch for training. If she did earn the chance to compete internationally, although Jordyn's expenses would be covered, we had to fund ourselves if we chose to go and watch her.

After reviewing all of the technical, emotional, psychological and financial aspects of elite gymnastics, we asked Jordyn what she wanted. She wanted to go for it. Our decision was made. We gave Jordyn our full support and told her that if she ever changed her mind and wanted to return to JO gymnastics, that was fine too. Nothing was permanent.

QUALIFYING AS AN INTERNATIONAL ELITE GYMNAST

The first step to becoming an elite gymnast is to qualify to be one. There are pre-elite and developmental programs that help gymnasts prepare to qualify to international elite status. Jordyn did not participate in any of these programs, but rather went straight to the qualifier events. A gymnast must be turning 11 years old in the year that she attempts to qualify. A junior elite gymnast is 15 or younger. Once a gymnast enters her 16th birth year, she becomes a senior elite gymnast.

For brand new "elites," qualification must take place at an official regional or national qualifying event. The USA Gymnastics website contains a schedule of these events. Gymnasts must qualify both in a compulsory and optional event. The compulsory qualifier has each gymnast doing the exact same skills on all four apparatus. The optional qualifying score, which is different for junior and senior international elites, must be obtained at a national qualifier event. Obtaining the scores in both compulsory and optional competitions, which may be attempted as many times as needed, qualifies the new international elite gymnast to the U.S. Classic. Jordyn qualified as an international elite gymnast in her first year and competed at the 2006 U.S. Classic. This meet serves as the qualifying event for the Visa Championships.

Not every gymnast meets criteria as an international elite gymnast in her first attempt or she may obtain scores high enough to qualify as an elite gymnast, but not earn the score needed to move on to the Visa Championships. These gymnasts have the choice to keep trying in the next season, or, if they haven't actually competed at the U.S. Classic, to petition to move back to JO status. It's not unusual for a gymnast to give the elite world a try and then move back to Level 10.

MAKING THE U.S. NATIONAL TEAM

The ultimate goal of any international elite gymnast is to be named to the U.S. National Team. In most situations, this is accomplished by performing well at the Visa Championships. Sometimes, previous members of the team, who are unable to compete in all four events at the Visa Championships, may be named to the team based on previous accomplishments. Typically, the top eight to 12 gymnasts in both the junior and senior levels are named to the U.S. National Team. The number of athletes varies each year depending on need.

Being a member of the U.S. National Team brings with it prestige, expectation and obligation. These are the gymnasts who will represent the U.S. in international competition. These gymnasts are the cream of the crop. National team members are expected to attend

2011 U.S. Women's Team

regularly scheduled camps held in Texas. Here the team not only trains together, but also vies for spots to compete at international meets. To be chosen to compete at a meet is considered an "assignment."

International competition provides invaluable experience. The gymnast learns a new level of independence. She must travel with the U.S. team, (parents can go to the competition but can't travel with the team), and compete in front of international judges. It's truly an experience of a lifetime.

Jordyn is in her sixth year as a member of the U.S. National Team. I believe this is something she is very proud of and takes very seriously. She has developed friendships with many of the girls on the team that will last a lifetime. As with anything in life that provides immense rewards and gratification, it comes with hard work and dedication.

college gymnastics

Elite gymnastics isn't typically the ultimate goal for most gymnasts. A full-ride athletic scholarship, on the other hand, is very attainable and rewarding to top Level 9 and 10 gymnasts. Currently there are 83 women's collegiate gymnastics programs that recruit gymnasts.

Collegiate gymnastics is different than club gymnastics. While there is an individual component, the success of the team comes first. Requirements and scoring are different than with club or JO gymnastics. There is a season that includes approximately 14 weekly meets. Best of all, it provides a great transition for your daughter to enter college with a sense of belonging and familiarity. As a collegiate athlete myself, I wouldn't trade that time in my life for anything.

COLLEGIATE RECRUITING

After winning the World Championships, Jordyn gave up her NCAA eligibility and our college recruiting days were abruptly over. That doesn't mean we didn't have a good taste of it. Jordyn started receiving collegiate materials in the mail when she was 10, as do many Level 10 gymnasts. With the advancement of the internet and video availability, college coaches can start following potential gymnasts very early in their JO careers. The NCAA has strict rules on communication with athletes and parents. By registering in the NCAA Eligibility Center for athletes, an athlete is abiding by all of these rules and not doing anything that would impede her scholarship eligibility.

Along our collegiate recruiting road, I was fortunate to get to know a few of the coaches. After she gave up her eligibility, I no longer had to abide by communication rules. At that time, I had the pleasure of getting to know Valerie Kondos-Field, long-time head coach for the University of California- Los Angeles gymnastics team. "Miss Val," as her adoring athletes call her, answered some questions for me on collegiate recruiting.

Q & A with Valerie Kondos-Field

Valerie Kondos Field was appointed head coach of the UCLA Bruins in 1991. She was selected by her peers as the NACGC/W National Coach of the Year in 1996, 1997, 2000 and 2001. She was also named the Pac-10 Coach of the Year in 1995, 2000, 2003 and 2012.

STARTING FOR THE RECRUITMENT PROCESS

RITA An athletic scholarship is often the ultimate goal for many upper level gymnasts. When should that pursuit begin and what steps should be taken to get the ball rolling?

MISS VAL A student-athlete becomes a recruitable student-athlete or "prospect" as soon as she enters her freshman year of high school. She should initiate the recruiting process at least by her sophomore year. She should send an e-mail to all of the schools she is interested in, even to those she doesn't know much about. In this e-mail she should introduce herself, include where she trains, how old she is, year in school, and at what level she competes. She should also include her home address, and any YouTube links that she has posted of her most recent gymnastics routines. The prospect needs to understand that the college coach can only reply by mail one time between a prospect's freshman and junior year in high school. Any further written correspondence is prohibited until September 1 of the prospect's junior year.

THE RECRUITING PROCESS

RITA Generally speaking, from the coach's perspective, how does the recruiting process work?

MISS VAL The recruiting process is different for every school. However, one thing remains similar, if a prospect shows enthusiasm and interest in learning more about our university and gymnastics program, she immediately gets herself on our radar.

RITA Is it necessary for parents to create a recruiting video of their athlete's skills and performances? What other steps can a parent take to assist in the recruiting process if their athlete is not being actively pursued?

MISS VAL: Links to YouTube videos are the easiest way for college coaches to assess athletes. I do not suggest producing videos with a lot of production time in them. All we need to see is the gymnast's current level of gymnastics, both in the gym training new skills and in competition. It is important to show competition links so we can assess how the prospect performs under pressure. Remember, it is always permissible for a parent or club coach to call a college coach to "pitch" a prospect.

THE RECUITED ATHLETE

RITA: **As a collegiate coach, what do you personally look for in an athlete that you are recruiting to your program?**

MISS VAL: Every college coach looks for different things; overall we're looking for a good "fit" with our university and our athletic program and the prospect.

THE NCAA ELIGIBILITY CENTER

RITA: **What is the NCAA Eligibility Center? When should athletes register in the clearing-house? Is that always necessary?**

MISS VAL: Every student-athlete in every sport who wants to attend college needs to be "cleared" by the NCAA Eligibility Center. I would suggest registering with the Eligibility Center in the prospect's sophomore year. They only have to pay the application fee once. It makes the final recruiting process a lot smoother if the prospect gets in the habit of forwarding her transcripts and test scores to the Eligibility Center whenever she get updated scores. During certain times of the year the Eligibility Center gets swamped, so if a prospect's file is kept up to date it could potentially help with any unexpected delays.

COMMUNICATING WITH THE COLLEGE COACH

RITA: **When can a college coach actually talk to a potential athlete? How does communication work before that time?**

MISS VAL: A college coach can call a prospect July 1 after her junior year in high school. A college coach can have in person contact with a prospect off-campus beginning July 15 after the prospect's junior year in high school. Before July 1, a prospect or her parents can call the college coach any time and as much as she would like, however if she leaves a message the college coach cannot call her back.

MISSING THE SCHOLARSHIP

RITA: **What's the biggest mistake you've seen potential collegiate gymnasts make that may have resulted in her not being given a scholarship?**

MISS VAL: There are a few mistakes I have seen happen a lot. One is a prospect only contacts a few collegiate programs and doesn't "cast a wide enough net." Or a prospect only looks into the schools that her friends are going to but really isn't a good fit for her. Another mistake is when a prospect or her parents don't ask enough questions because they either haven't done their homework or they feel that it isn't their place to ask certain questions. Recruits, their parents and coaches should feel free to ask any question that comes to mind. This is probably the biggest decision the prospect has made in her young life. It's a big deal and she should accumulate as much information as possible before making a decision.

SCHOLARSHIP TERM

RITA: **Are scholarships a four-year guarantee or are they renewed every year based on performance?**

MISS VAL: There is no such thing as a four-year scholarship. A coach can tell a prospect that we are prepared to renew your scholarship each year provided you meet certain criteria.

THE FULL-RIDE

RITA: **Are all college gymnastics scholarships full-rides or can they be partial?**

MISS VAL: Most college gymnastics scholarships are full-rides, however, a college program CAN divide scholarship money up, but the program cannot have more than 12 student-athletes on scholarship in any given year, unless the additional student-athletes are "injured-retired."

RITA: **Many gymnasts verbally commit to a gymnastics scholarship in the fall of their junior year of high school. Is it too late if you haven't obtained a scholarship by then?**

MISS VAL: The timeline to verbally commit depends on the prospect. My suggestion is to ask the coach a lot of questions pertaining to the offered position. Remember, no question is off limits.

KEEPING THE SCHOLARSHIP

RITA: **How important is performance in the junior and senior year of high school once a scholarship has been accepted?**

MISS VAL: This is a personal question per coach; however, I would venture to say that the prospect's performance in her junior and senior years is extremely important. We, in the gymnastics community, pride ourselves on the fact that more times than not we honor our verbal commitments. However, the prospect should understand that she is expected to maintain the gymnastics and fitness level at which she was recruited in order to expect the university coach to honor the verbal commitment.

high school gymnastics

Club gymnastics is an intense commitment but it's not the only option for enjoying the sport of gymnastics. High school gymnastics can be the perfect option for gymnasts who love the sport so much they don't want to quit, yet aren't interested in committing to the demands of club gymnastics. Not every high school has a gymnastics team. Providing the sport at the high school level requires the purchase of expensive equipment and mats, allocating room and time for training, and hiring a coach with the proper qualifications.

The difficulty of skills performed at the high school level is typically less than that of club gymnastics. There are no designated levels, but there may be more than one division to separate ability levels. Scores are still based on the 10-point scale, but criteria for deductions and bonus may be different. The main draw to high school gymnastics is the reduced time commitment. In high school, gymnastics is a seasonal sport. Year-round training is not organized. With the lower difficulty level, college recruiting is typically focused on club gymnastics. That said, a club gymnast who retires from the club and participates in high school gymnastics might still remain a collegiate interest.

One perk of high school gymnastics is the recognition athletes receive from their school and community as opposed to gymnasts in club gymnastics. Many local newspapers are reluctant to cover club sports due to time and space constraints. So the high school gymnastics state meet, for example, might be worthy of a front page of the sports section, while the state meet for club gymnastics doesn't get mentioned.

retiring from the sport of gymnastics

Gymnastics isn't really considered a lifetime fitness sport like running, cycling, swimming or other recreational activities. At some point flexibility begins to decrease, and it is more difficult and dangerous to perform the complex maneuvers. That's not to say it's impossible.

Despite its obvious addicting tendencies, the sport of gymnastics does come to an end for all athletes. Whether it's a premature ending due to long-term injuries or just the natural progression of life, the end of gymnastics is part of life.

WHEN TO RETIRE FROM GYMNASTICS

For gymnasts who truly love the sport and continue all the way through collegiate gymnastics, the end of that era is natural and expected. But for many, the decision to retire from the sport is difficult and melancholy. It's often difficult for parents to accept their child quitting the sport, especially if the gymnast was talented and successful.

THE BODY RULES

Two years ago I was hit by a car going 40 mph doing what I love most, running. While I could have been badly hurt, I survived with only a few injuries. I had a laceration to the back of my head, a neck injury leaving me with chronic pain, a broken fibula and a torn ACL in my knee. I was lucky to be alive. The broken leg and subsequent knee surgery kept me away from running for months. I couldn't believe the deep emotional toll that had on my psyche despite knowing it was only a temporary setback. That experience gave me increased empathy for anyone who is unable to participate in a loved activity due to injury. When I see gymnasts attempt to return to the sport after major injuries, I am not surprised. It's hard to be forced to give up something you love.

There are times, however, when the cons of returning far outweigh the pros. Parents need to look at the long-term effects of injuries and the wear and tear gymnastics has on the body. Structurally, we are not all created equal. Repetitive motions and impact on muscles, joints and bones are not the same for everyone. Despite smart coaching, proper and safe equipment and knowledgeable medical care, not every body can tolerate gymnastics. At the point of risking chronic lifelong pain, hard decisions must be made. The decision to retire from gymnastics due to chronic injury is always difficult, especially when the gymnast doesn't want to quit. It is not a decision that should be made hastily, but only after careful consideration with the gymnast, parents, coaches and even the physician. There can be other options for an athlete with a deep love for gymnastics that allows her to stay involved in the sport, whether it be through coaching, a career in sports medicine, or becoming a future gym owner.

THE MOM RULES

It's very common for gymnasts to go through periods of frustration and want to leave the sport. At what point do you realize that your child might actually want to quit gymnastics? This is a very delicate matter. Gymnastics is not a seasonal sport. Taking time off will affect progress. Sometimes a break is needed to validate the desire of the gymnast to quit the sport. Many will realize that they miss it too much and return. Others will move on quickly to other sports and never look back.

It's up to the parent to listen to the gymnast. If the reason for her change of heart is legitimate, let her move on. If it seems to be a whim based on a few bad days of practice, a punishment from a coach or a fight with a fellow gymnast, deal with the root of the problem before making a huge decision.

It's important to realize that no decision has to be permanent. I've seen gymnasts leave the sport for two to three years and then return and do very well. I've also seen gymnasts be forced to participate in gymnastics and wind up bitter and hostile. Remember, the role of the parent is to provide opportunities and offer support.

THE GYMNAST RULES

Through observations as a gym mom, I have decided that there is often a "hump" year that determines if a gymnast will remain in club gymnastics or not. Typically, the "hump" year is around eighth or ninth grade- a time when high school life can pull like a magnet. Decision points that arise for the gymnast at this time include:

- Do I love gymnastics enough do it exclusively and forego participating in other high school sports?

- Do I want to pursue collegiate gymnastics?

- Am I on track to pursue a college scholarship?

- Is high school gymnastics an option?

- Am I willing to give up certain high school events, such as prom or spring break that may coincide with the state, regional or national championship meets?

As previously mentioned, no decision is carved in stone. A gymnast who is on the fence about deciding to retire or continue can always do a "trial separation." Compromises can be made. I have seen gymnasts choose to skip meets or trips to attend a once-in-a-lifetime high school event. Again, a conversation with the coach and some creative flexibility may keep everyone happy.

it's all worth it

In speaking with hundreds of gymnasts over the years, and especially in preparation for this book, I did not encounter a single athlete who regretted her years as a gymnast. Current gymnasts talked about their gymnastics life with enthusiasm and spirit. Former gymnasts treasure their time in the sport they loved. The key, I found, to those who had the fondest memories was an experience filled with mutual respect with coaches and parents. The ups of the sport brought profound gratification and pride and the down periods allowed for lessons and growth. All of it- the periods of joy and pride, frustration and disappointment – all of it is worth every moment.

WHAT GYMNASTS AND GYM MOMS
SAID ABOUT LIFE WITH GYMNASTICS

Q: What was the biggest benefit of being a gymnast?

A: In the simplest of answers…it made me who I am today. It is the best classroom for teaching about life. Focus, determination, and hard work *do* really lead to success. When you fail, you have learned something, and you get up and try, try again.

Sometimes in life, you are going to have people (i.e. coaches, teammates, bosses and co-workers, husbands and children) that you get irritated with or are difficult or you really, really don't like some days, but figure out how to work with those people and you get the job done.

There is nothing more bonding than pouring out sweat and tears with teammates, going through ups and downs, and going after goals together. Teammates are forever my best friends in life.

Heather Cooper, Former Gymnast, Lansing, Michigan

A: Perseverance! Learning how to overcome obstacles to achieve your dreams helps develop so many skills that will last a lifetime.

Tonya Toonen, Gym mom

A: Gymnastics has given me a sense of discipline that has transferred to all aspects of my life because as a gymnast I was trained at a very young age to live disciplined lifestyle. That discipline not only applied to my training and competition, but I also notice it applies to my time management skills and ability to follow through with assignments and tasks in the real world.

Tasha Schwikert, 2000 Olympic bronze medalist

A: There are many things I loved about being a gymnast. The self-confidence, motivation, determination, and focus that I learned have helped me through school and achieving goals outside of gymnastics, in high school, through college, and now my job and extracurricular activities. I think that my most favorite thing about being a gymnast is the self-awareness of my own body. Not everyone gets the chance to get to know his or her own body at such a deep level. When you reach a certain level in gymnastics where your body has to be in top condition you feel and learn to use muscles that you never thought existed. It is beneficial later in life when I feel aches or pains I know exactly where its coming from and can use this knowledge to help others. This awareness sparked my interest in anatomy and biology, and I went on to major in biology and will hopefully be going to medical school in the near future.

Gigja, Former Gymnast

CHAPTER TEN
reflection

A s the word of my book project became public, many questioned why I was writing it before the 2012 Olympics. After reading this book you know that it is not a story about Jordyn and the Olympics. Rather, it is a story of my experience as a gym mom through the years of recreational, compulsory, optional and elite gymnastics. I wanted to share what I learned about the wonderful world of gymnastics via this informative guide for parents of gymnasts.

My story, from the perspective of the mother of an Olympic hopeful gymnast, is one of reflection more than information. Jordyn's gymnastics success has changed my life more in the last six months than I ever dreamed possible.

keep things in perspective

It's almost ironic how every now and then, when I'm almost irrationally fixated on some relatively small problem in my life, something brings me back down to earth. As a registered nurse in the emergency department of a Level 1 trauma center, I've seen my share of tragedy and sadness. There was the 28 year-old mother of a four-week old baby diagnosed with lung cancer; the woman with a headache who had a brain tumor; the young man who suffered an aneurysm on the golf course; and the four-month old baby who died of SIDS. There are patients with no health insurance, no job, no home, and no family. I see it often and it humbles me. My life is full of blessings. We are all healthy, my husband and I are both employed and we live in a safe, free country.

When Jordyn suffered her ankle injury at the 2010 Visa Championships, I caught myself feeling sad and disappointed. It didn't seem fair.

Why did she get hurt at such an inopportune time? For a few days, nothing seemed that great. I was so consumed with my feelings of frustration and letdown it began to carry over into all aspects of my life. A couple of weeks later, while work in the emergency room, I was quickly brought back to reality. A woman about my age checked in with a fever. She had end-stage breast cancer. Her hair was gone due to effects of chemotherapy. Her face was moon-shaped from the steroid medication. I suddenly felt very superficial and selfish. I spent the last two weeks full of bitterness and disappointment over Jordyn's recent misfortune. My daughter tried her hardest and deserved my support and encouragement, not my negativity and bitterness. Injuries heal. Life would go on for us. The outlook is not optimistic for everyone. A few weeks after seeing that ill woman, I saw her obituary in our local paper. I have learned over the past several years to remind myself daily of just how blessed I am. With or without gymnastics, I am blessed!

provide unconditional support

I will never forget sitting in the stands at a football game last fall when my son was the starting quarterback for our high school team. After throwing an incomplete pass, I heard a spectator yell, "What the heck was that, you've got to be kidding me. Come on Wieber, get it together." My heart sunk knowing that someone was disappointed in my son. He was out on the field with a tough defensive opponent trying his hardest to make a play work. How could someone yell something so mean?

We all want to see our children succeed, in sports, school, and life but there will be bumps in the road. There will be disappointments and failures. Many times it's those situations that build character, teach lessons and create growth. Children need to see the face of support and encouragement from parents, not disappointment or judgment. It's easy to get wrapped up in winning and lose sight of the real benefit of competitive sports- the development of a strong work ethic and taking on a challenge.

count it all joy

As a special education major back in the early eighties, I spent a summer working at a school for the severely physically and mentally disabled. At 20 years old, I became profoundly aware of the struggles and challenges faced by these students and their families. I remember spending almost an hour preparing the students to swim in the therapeutic pool. This included changing diapers and dressing full-grown young adults, negotiating their rigid limbs into the adaptive equipment and floating them around the warm pool. They would squeal with joy at this seemingly trivial activity that I took for granted. That experience stuck with me over the years and has greatly impacted my appreciation for having healthy children.

Whether I am watching my children on the playground, the soccer field or on a world stage in gymnastics, I am always mindful of how grateful I am that they are able to experience the joy of physical activity and competitive sports.

When all is said and done, I want to look back and know that I provided my children with opportunities for growth in sports. Any success they may achieve is a bonus.

final thoughts

Looking back now, I realize, regardless of what happens in the months to come between the printing of this book and the 2012 Olympics, our life is about to change again. The years of our familiar and comfortable gymnastics routine will eventually come to an end. It's bittersweet in many ways. The past 12 years would have been much easier with a crystal ball showing the final outcome of Jordyn's career. The next months will surely change our lives again no matter what happens. The bottom line is, it's all been worth it! Every moment of joy and pride, every moment of frustration and disappointment– it's all been part of what has directed us, and shaped us into the family we are today.

I have spoken these words to Jordyn many, many times and they are the truth: "I love you. Even without gymnastics, you amaze me. If you told me you wanted to quit tomorrow, I am proud of what you have accomplished, what you have learned from the sport, and the person you are. Your life is your dream, and I am here to support you in whatever direction you take."